"Adam McHugh has been a significant contributor to the conversation about how introverts experience the world. His new book, *The Listening Life*, has the power to reshape how both introverts and extroverts make space for deep listening in a world that swims in the shallows. Highly recommended."

Susan Cain, cofounder of Quiet Revolution, author of *Quiet*

"Listening is one of the best gifts we can give or receive. Listening changes things. Listening, the way Adam McHugh describes it, could just change the world."

Ruth Haley Barton, founder and president, Transforming Center, author of *Life Together in Christ*

"*The Listening Life* is the kind of book that made me at times not want to turn the page—because I needed to! What the book did was still my soul and remind me to be still before God—to silence the noise and open the closed doors to hear. In hearing we learn that in listening to God and to one another we enter into the graces of love. On every page Adam McHugh offers wisdom that slowly marches us into a deeper kind of life, one marked by listening to God in a way that teaches us how to listen to one another and to ourselves. There are two kinds of people: those who talk and those who listen—the former need to read this book slowly and listen well to the lesson about reverse listening, while the latter will discover fresh light on a discipline now deepened."

Scot McKnight, Julius R. Mantey Professor in New Testament, Northern Seminary

"If it were possible to combine the voices of Dallas Willard, N. D. Wilson and Jim Gaffigan, then what you would get is Adam S. McHugh. His writing is profound, lyrical and self-deprecating in all the right ways. There are few books I want to start again once I've finished. *The Listening Life* is now one of them. I adore this stunning, important book and want to give it to everyone I know."

Emily P. Freeman, author of *Simply Tuesday*

"Adam McHugh is a voice worth listening to. His new book will be a gift to anyone who wants to cultivate what Jesus called 'ears to hear.'"

John Ortberg, senior pastor of Menlo Park Presbyterian Church

THE
LISTENING
LIFE

EMBRACING ATTENTIVENESS
in a **WORLD** *of* **DISTRACTION**

Adam S. McHugh

IVP Books

An imprint of InterVarsity Press
Downers Grove, Illinois

InterVarsity Press
P.O. Box 1400, Downers Grove, IL 60515-1426
ivpress.com
email@ivpress.com

InterVarsity Press® is the book-publishing division of InterVarsity Christian Fellowship/USA®, a movement
of students and faculty active on campus at hundreds of universities, colleges and schools of nursing in the
United States of America, and a member movement of the International Fellowship of Evangelical Students.
For information about local and regional activities, visit intervarsity.org.

Scripture quotations, unless otherwise noted, are from the New Revised Standard Version of the Bible,
copyright 1989 by the Division of Christian Education of the National Council of the Churches of Christ in
the USA. Used by permission. All rights reserved.

While any stories in this book are true, some names and identifying information may have been changed to
protect the privacy of individuals.

Published in association with the literary agency of WordServe Literary Group, Ltd., wordserveliterary.com.

Cover design: David Fassett
Interior design: Beth McGill

Images: © Creativeye99/iStockphoto

ISBN 978-0-8308-4412-8 (print)
ISBN 978-0-8308-7969-4 (digital)

Printed in the United States of America ∞

Library of Congress Cataloging-in-Publication Data
McHugh, Adam S., 1976-
  The listening life : embracing attentiveness in a world of distraction / Adam S. McHugh.
    pages cm
  Includes bibliographical references.
  ISBN 978-0-8308-4412-8 (pbk. : alk. paper)
  1. Listening--Religious aspects--Christianity. 2. Attention--Religious aspects--Christianity. 3. Distraction
(Psychology)--Religious aspects. I. Title.
  BV4647.L56M34 2015
  248.4--dc23

                                                                                        2015033921

P 22 21 20 19 18 17 16 15 14 13 12 11 10 9 8 7 6 5 4

Y 34 33 32 31 30 29 28 27 26 25 24 23 22 21 20 19 18 17

For Mark Roberts, Steve Stuckey and Donna Herrick—

three people who taught me how to be a listener, by listening to me.

Contents

Introduction

LISTENING COMES FIRST. In this life, you listen even before you are aware of it. From within the womb an unborn child is already listening to the voices of her parents. After her birth, she will spend the next months hearing the words they speak, whisper and sing to her, until one day she will start echoing those words, one imperfect syllable at a time.

To master a foreign language we must hear it spoken by others before we can reproduce the sounds our ears have heard. Virtuoso musicians in their early years are immersed in music, hearing the chord progressions and melodies that will lodge in their souls and, one day, sound from their instruments. Much of our formative years is spent in classrooms listening to teachers, in homes listening to our parents and in church listening to the stories the Bible tells us.

When we meet the primeval universe in Genesis, we learn that it is unformed and chaotic but that somehow it has an ear, because its first action is to listen to the Voice that pierces the darkness. God commands light and the cosmos hears and obeys, and through its acts of listening, order and harmony supplant the watery abyss. Six days into the making of this listening world, God creates the first humans, and their original act is to hear the blessing to populate the earth with other image-bearers and God-listeners.

Listening is foundational to what it means to be human.

Throughout the Bible listening is the central act of the people of God. They are those who are gathered and formed by his voice and held together by his word. They hear his promises and judgments, instructions and warnings, reassurances and exhortations.

The centerpiece of Israel's prayer life, the Shema, begins with the word *hear*: "Hear, O Israel: The LORD our God, the LORD is one" (Deuteronomy 6:4 NIV). The Hebrew word *shema* means "hear." Jewish children are instructed to rehearse these words as they rise in the morning and as they fall asleep. From dawn until dusk their lives are made by listening.

You become a disciple by hearing. Listening is the first act of discipleship as fishermen drop their nets and follow when Jesus calls, and listening is the core of their apprenticeship as they listen their way from Galilee to Jerusalem. Paul reminds us that hearing must come before faith, indeed that faith proceeds from hearing. How can someone believe, he presses, in someone they have never heard of? "So faith comes from what is heard, and what is heard comes through the word of Christ" (Romans 10:17). The apostle James famously counsels his hearers to be quick to listen, slow to speak (James 1:19). Ancient wisdom cautions us that "if one gives answer before hearing, it is folly and shame" (Proverbs 18:13). This is the pattern that life commands. Listen before you speak. Learn before you teach. Hear the call before you lead. Absorb the word before you preach it.

But somewhere along the way we start to violate the natural order of things. Speaking our minds and asserting ourselves take priority over listening. We interrupt someone else because we are convinced we already know what he or she is going to say. We begin to take up more space than we allow for others. We consider ourselves experts on topics without anything more to learn. We tell

God what to give rather than asking what God wants to give. We participate by speaking and sharing, and we assert our identities by taking verbal stands. We shout our messages from the rooftops without knowing who is listening and what they need. We view others as projects rather than people with unique stories to be heard. We consider our great Christian task to be preaching, rather than assuming the listening posture of a servant. We speak volumes, but we listen in snippets.

When this reversal of the pattern persists, we find ourselves building lives that shelter us from having to truly listen. We may move into churches and neighborhoods full of people whose views parallel our own, avoiding the dissonance created by contrasting voices by constructing theological and social echo chambers. We crystallize our beliefs and cease to ask questions. The great hope of the Internet has been that dialogue will prevail, that people with different theologies, worldviews and politics will log in to learn, grow and communicate with those who disagree with them. Yet it would seem that social media has helped people connect with like-minded people, and the unfortunate consequence has been the intensifying and radicalizing of beliefs and the deeper entrenchment of people's beliefs. We settle into our own little truth corners.

What the Bible portrays as a household of faith instead becomes a scattering of encampments, people who warm themselves by their own fires, whoop with their own war cries, listen solely to their appointed leaders and only interact with the other camps when firing arrows.

Psychology professor David Benner says that a major obstacle to growth in our listening abilities is that most of us already think that we're good listeners.[1] This book is predicated on the assumption that most of us are *not* good listeners. Therapists I know say that many of their clients meet with them simply because they are not being listened to in their most important relationships. Without diminishing the value of professional therapy, I would argue that the fact that we pay millions of dollars annually for people to listen to us indicates our poverty in this arena. Everyone is talking, but so few people are truly being heard.

We need to learn how to listen because all the talking in the world will not make our relationships what we want them to be, and it will not make us into the sort of people we want to be. Our longings for intimacy will not be satisfied through one-way conversations and interactions that feel like competitions. Our desire to be transformed will not be met through giving voice to all the noise in our souls. Our identities will not be discovered in finding our own voice independent of others but in helping others find their voices.

We learn how to listen because we want to learn how to love. We want to learn how to practice hospitality, how to truly welcome people into our lives. We want to be story-hearers and not just storytellers. We want to find the internal quiet and stillness that will open us to being changed. We want to learn how to listen because we want to become more human.

I didn't get serious about listening until I realized I wasn't good looking enough to get women to pay attention to me any other way. I am not proud to admit this. In college I borrowed a copy of *Men Are from Mars, Women Are from Venus* from a friend.[2] Actually, I took it from her dorm room without telling her because I was embarrassed to be reading it. I still have it. In that book I learned that women are listeners and men are problem solvers. I would later dismiss that as a gender stereotype, but at the time I used it to stop trying to fix everything and just be with people. I wooed women with eye contact, paraphrasing and active listening sounds.

Listening at the start of a relationship is easy. In the early months there is no way you can anticipate future conversations when you sit gripping the arms of your chair, teeth marks on your tongue, summoning all your will power to keep from interrupting someone saying something you disagree with. In those moments the God-given ratio of two ears to one mouth seems highly unjust. But that is when the work of true listening really begins. It's one thing to listen at the beginning of our relationships, but it's another thing entirely to *continue* to practice the discipline of listening before you speak.

The question that drives this book is, how would our relationships change, and how would we change, if we approached every situation with the intention of listening first? What if we approached our relationship with God as listeners? What if we viewed our relationship with nature as one of listening? What if we approached our relationships using our ears rather than our mouths? What if we sought to listen to our emotions before we preached to them?

Even though listening has been central to my ministries as pastor, chaplain and spiritual director, the listening message is one that I still need. They say that pastors preach the sermon they most need to hear, and I am writing this book because I need to hear it myself. I need to remind myself that nothing has changed me like listening. It has not simply been the content that I have received through listening—the words, stories and whispers of others—that has changed me; it is the very act of listening. There is something about settling in and paying attention to someone, or Someone, letting them have the floor and steer the conversation where they want to go, that is in itself transformative.

The very first word of the Rule of St. Benedict, that famous text that has guided the life of monastic communities since the sixth century, is *listen*. I want for us to put listening back where it belongs, at the beginning, in every aspect of life and faith. Listening isn't only something we do in the preparatory stages of life, as though it's a phase we grow out of once we reach a certain age. Nor is it just a pleasant medicine that we need to inject a little more of into our relationships. Listening ought to be at the heart of our spirituality, our relationships, our mission as the body of Christ, our relationship to culture and the world. We are invited to approach everything with the goal of listening first. We are called to participate in the listening life.

ONE

The Listening Life

YOUR LIST OF LIFE-CHANGING BOOKS probably doesn't include an etymological dictionary. That takes a peculiar kind of nerdiness that few want to claim. Yet I confess that one of the most significant lessons I learned was from an etymological dictionary, that hefty resource that breaks down the origins of words. I'm pretty sure the unabridged edition I dropped onto a library table splintered the legs underneath it, but soon it began to repair some cracks that existed in my mind. Before I opened it, with the help of a burly librarian, I knew that listening has the power to heal divisions. It can bridge the divide between people in conflict, transform stalemates into learning opportunities and unearth solutions from seemingly intractable situations. But I had no idea that listening can heal the rift between those proverbial enemies *hearing* and *doing*.

Those bitter rivals are pitted against each other in a few Scriptures, with doing billed as the heavy favorite. Paul says it's not those who *hear* the law but those who *do* the law who are righteous. James warns those hearers who deceive themselves into thinking they don't need to be doers. Jesus concludes his Sermon on the Mount by comparing people who hear his words but don't act on them to a house built on sand.

Here are clear warnings that hearing by itself cannot be trusted and that doing is the badge of the faithful. It would seem that hearing is but a narrow channel pouring into the deep sea of doing. Yet the etymological dictionary taught me that the sharp distinction between hearing and doing is the result of human beings tearing asunder what belongs together. For this is its lesson: the words *listen* and *obey* have the same root. In Latin, the word "obey" would not exist without the word "listen." The word we translate into English as "obedience" literally means a "listening from below." Obedience is a deep listening, a listening of the whole person, a hearing with your ears and with your heart and with your arms and legs.

This etymological thrill ride does not stop with Latin. The deep connection between listening and obedience also appears in Greek and Hebrew, the primary languages of the Bible. The biblical words for "listen" or "hear" can just as easily be translated, and frequently are, as "obey" or "give heed to." Plus, the root for the words translated in the Greek New Testament as "obey" and "obedience" is—you guessed it—*listen*. Listening and obedience are inextricably, unabashedly linked, so much so that we can say that those who don't act on what they hear have not actually listened. As seminary professor Howard Hendricks put it, "Biblically speaking, to hear and not to do is not to hear at all."[1]

LISTENING AS OBEDIENCE

The interplay between listening and obedience expresses itself in our lives all the time. Sound has the ability to "command" us, to summon a response in us, forcing us to take notice. Unlike visual stimuli, certain sounds have an invasive, inescapable quality to them, and we don't have "earlids" to protect us from them.[2] Our sense of hearing is the alarm system of our bodies. As neuroscientist Seth Horowitz writes, our brains process threatening sounds in a tenth of a second, "elevating your heart rate, hunching your shoulders and making you cast around to see if whatever you heard is going to pounce and eat you."[3] Our bodies involuntarily respond to, or obey, particular sounds. Someone screams in pain and our bodies jerk instantly in their direction. An ambulance siren behind us has us moving to the side of the road almost instinctually. The sound of a jackhammer disrupts our train of thought, invading our world without permission. Sound calls us to attention.[4] When someone says our name in a loud and crowded room, even if they are not talking to us, we turn toward them. And then there is music. A song sweeps us up with its melody so that we can't *not* be moved by it. We all know the power music has to shape our moods and stir our emotions, even causing us to make decisions and take action. Music becomes an imperative that our bodies and emotions respond to. Dance is our obedience to music.

In our everyday speech, we regularly communicate that listening involves more than the sense of hearing. The complaint I hear most from parents is that their children don't listen to them. My friend Mark has a spirited two-year-old named Will who, as Mark reports, "is in the phase of asserting his independence from us by doing the exact opposite of what we say. It's harder to get him to listen now." When parents say their children won't listen to them, they mean they won't obey them. Or who of us hasn't sat in the driver's seat, taken a route different from that recommended by the person next to us, gotten lost and later heard, "You should have listened to me!" Meaning, "You should have done what I told you to do." No one said listening was always fun.

Psychologist and marriage researcher John Gottman says that one of the leading gauges for measuring a happy marriage is whether spouses allow themselves to be influenced by the other person.[5] Are they changed by their relationship, or do they become more entrenched in their old ways? Being influenced by another person is a sure indication of true listening because it means that your choices and actions are following your ears. Apparently, listening is important in marriage. Who knew?

New Testament scholar Scot McKnight reports that the word *listen* appears in the Bible over fifteen hundred times and that the most frequently voiced complaint in the Bible is that the people don't listen.[6] Isaiah 48:8 is particularly scathing:

> You have never heard, you have never known,
>   from of old your ear has not been opened.

> For I knew that you would deal very treacherously,
>   and that from birth you were called a rebel.

When your ears are closed, you do not yield to God's commands, and you are called a rebel.

Listening is never passive, a stall or placeholder until doing steps in and saves the day. Biblical listening is a whole-hearted, full-bodied listening that not only vibrates our eardrums but echoes in our souls and resonates out into our limbs. John's famous picture of Jesus as the Word of God means that Jesus' entire incarnated life, not only his parables and sermons, is the expression of God's mind. His life is God's speech to us. We are correspondingly asked to listen with our lives, and we are not truly listening unless we are responding to Jesus with all our heart, mind, soul and strength. This kind of listening is done on the move.

HEARING AND LISTENING

Up until now I have been using *hearing* and *listening* interchangeably, and for the sake of ease I will go back and forth between those two words throughout this book. The Bible does not sharply distinguish between the two, though I suspect that when the Lord says through the prophet Isaiah "keep on hearing, but do not understand" (Isaiah 6:9 ESV), he is making a distinction. Hearing, generally speaking, is one of the five senses, the one that centers on our ears and our brain's processing of the sounds it receives. It is involuntary and momentary. Hearing is something that happens to us. Sounds force our attention, and we "obey" them instinctually through our body's responses.

Listening, on the other hand, is something that we choose. Listening is a practice of focused attention. Hearing is an act of the senses, but listening is an act of the will. In listening you center not only your ears but also your mind, heart and posture on someone or something other than yourself. It is a chosen obedience, like soldiers falling into line the moment their commanding officer calls them to attention.

THE URGENCY OF LISTENING

Listening is often presented as a balm for making our relationships go more smoothly and peacefully, for making us more aware of the needs of people around us. The interpersonal reasons are valuable and essential, but I think there are also deep intrapersonal reasons for learning how to listen. When listening has been hard, these personal motivations are what have kept me going. I have devoted and redevoted myself to listening because it is making me into the kind of person I wish to be.

The beginning of discipleship is listening. At the sound of Jesus' voice, his first followers dropped their nets and followed him. Of course, discipleship must involve more than one episode of listening; it is an ongoing journey of listening. Disciples are walking listeners. If we think that discipleship is lacking in today's church, then perhaps we should place an emphasis on people learning how to listen.

Listening is important enough to Jesus that he devotes his first parable to it (Mark 4:1-20). In Mark's Gospel Jesus frames the parable of the sower with the opening word "Listen!" and the closing exclamation "Let anyone with ears to hear listen!" Overtly about a farmer indiscriminately scattering seed on different types of soil, the story is actually about different types of hearers. There are the path hearers—those who don't really hear at all, deflecting and dismissing Jesus' words. There are the rocky listeners, who let the word penetrate a little but then reject it because of adverse voices of struggle and persecution. Third are the thorny listeners, who listen a while longer but slowly allow the subtle power of se-ductive voices—the accumulation of wealth and the sparkle of ma-terial things—to suffocate the word. Finally are the true and fruitful listeners, those who receive the word deep into themselves, where it does its proper work of flowering and bearing fruit.

This last group would seem to be the ones who, in Jesus' words, have "ears to hear," by which he seems to link listening and com-prehension, treating ears as organs of understanding. Those with hearing ears have a level of attunement to the deeper meanings embedded in Jesus' teaching. Later in Mark's Gospel Jesus cautions his followers to be careful about how they listen, because how they listen will determine how much they understand.

What seems to separate the different types of listeners is the amount of effort that they put into listening. What we lack in under-standing we can make up for in asking questions. The true listeners are those who stay, who crowd around Jesus and ask him the inter-pretation of the parable. This is the kind of listener God desires: those who pursue and seek and relentlessly question. They sit with Jesus' words like an old friend that you know yet really don't know, chewing and digesting, continuing to seek greater clarity and depth of under-standing. They don't just ask the first question; they also ask the second and third questions. They exhaust others with their questions.

As has been noted by many biblical scholars, the parable of the sower not only describes different types of hearers, but it leads to the very divisions it describes. Jesus' parables sift out those who are hard of hearing, who merely want to be entertained and see the new rabbinic celebrity. Those hearers scatter after Jesus finishes teaching while the true listeners stay.

I taught this parable to college students for years, and I marveled at how our classroom setting would inevitably mirror the original setting of the parable. After the class was over, most students would head back to the dorms, but there would be one or two students who stayed and asked question after question or wrote on their manuscripts, laboring to understand what Jesus was saying and the implications it had for their lives. I always wondered whether these were the students with ears to hear.

Listening makes us into disciples—those who learn, who follow and who submit to the Lord. And listening also makes us into servants. What is a servant if not an obedient listener? We could rephrase Jesus' famous words about servanthood like this and keep his same meaning: "You know that the Gentile rulers tell people what to do, and their great ones expect to be heard. It is not so among you; whoever wishes to be great must listen, and whoever wishes to be first among you must be listener to all" (see Mark 10:42-43). In Jesus' upside-down kingdom, the tables are turned. Those in the position to tell people what to do must become listeners. In the Gentile world, listening flows from the bottom up, but in Jesus' kingdom, listening is top-down.

Too often we try to gain control with our words. Listening, done well, gives power away. A commitment to listening is one of the best antidotes for power and privilege. A servant listener does not dominate the conversation. Servants take the attention off themselves and focus their attention on the needs and interests of others. The call to servanthood is at the heart of the gospel; it is the call to humble ourselves, to empty ourselves of our own agendas and egos and submit ourselves to the Lord and to others. Servant listening is a practice of presence, in which we set aside what might distract us and what we think should happen in a moment or conversation. It is an act of humility, in which we acknowledge that no matter who we are listening to, we come to learn. Servant listening is an act of surrender, in which we lay down our verbal weapons, our preconceived notions, our quick advice and our desire to steer the conversation toward ourselves. We release our grasp on the terms and direction of the conversation.

We love to talk about listening. It's easier than actually listening. There is much lip service paid to listening, but listening is a service of the ear, the mind and the heart. Listening is an act of servanthood, and serving is hard. There are no accolades in serving. When a servant is doing his job, no one notices. If we wish to imitate Jesus and become servants, we must learn how to listen.

TOO MANY VOICES

Things were getting weird. Jesus had dragged a few of his disciples up the hill, and though he climbed the mountain with his normal face, Jesus now wore his mountain face: bleach-white, sparkling like a diamond in the sun. Then some uninvited, strangely familiar guests had crashed the party, men that seemed a little too comfortable on mountaintops with glowing faces. But Peter, unfazed as always in the face of drama, hatched a plan. "Lord," he said, "this is the most epic reunion in history—you and Moses and Elijah having drinks and talking about old times. So what if James and John and I build you some tents to keep this party going?" Then followed an awkward silence of biblical proportions.

Fortunately, a talking cloud made the situation less weird. It swept over them, and from within a voice thundered: "This is my Son, the one that I love, and you must listen to him!" And Moses and Elijah called it an early night (see Mark 9:1-8).

Even with all the visual theatrics and prophetic cameos in the transfiguration, the story is ultimately about listening. Specifically, it is about *who* we should be listening to. The first voice we must listen to belongs to Jesus, because his voice has divine credentials. We must be careful about how we listen, because life in this world is wildly polyphonic, filled with countless voices that beckon us to do their bidding.

I had a memorable lunch a few years ago with my friends Mike and Claudia, who had recently returned from Malawi, a small country in southeastern Africa. We were sitting in a booth at one of those chain restaurants that has a twenty-seven-page menu. That booth was my front-row seat to culture shock. Mike and Claudia picked up the menu and quickly developed the pro-verbial African-wildebeest-in-headlights glaze. The server came and went several times, trying to take our orders, but Mike and Claudia could not make a decision, paralyzed by the sheer variety of options. Claudia explained, "In Malawi, you have your choice of chicken or chicken. There are just so many choices here! Every-thing sounds so good."

We have an infinite buffet of options, and everything sounds so good. Whether we realize it or not, we are persistently serenaded by a cacophony of voices that battle for our souls, each seducing us with promises of fullness. Marketing experts say that Americans living in large cities are exposed to as many as five thousand adver-tisements per day.[7] In such a world, we have the freedom to be the ultimate selective listeners. If one voice doesn't deliver what it promised, we can always listen to another voice that offers us more satisfaction. As a result, our attention spans become shorter and our tastes become more fastidious and demanding. We can become consumers who are impossible to please because we think that there is always a more appealing voice speaking somewhere else, promising us more happiness.

The sort of people that we become is, in large part, determined by the voices that we choose to listen to. Truly, we do not have a choice of listening versus not listening. We all obey certain voices, and thus the question is not "Will I listen?" but "Which voices will I listen to?" But it is not only a matter of choosing to listen to good voices over bad ones. If only it were as simple as the proverbial whispering angel and devil on our shoulders. It is also a matter of whether we will choose to listen to *different* voices, voices that don't sound the same as our own. Will we listen to the voices of different cultures, ethnicities, backgrounds and beliefs? Will we listen to the voices that unsettle us and might make us feel anxious or guilty? If we choose to listen only to voices that echo our own, we will be limited in our growth and stunted in our spirituality. Choosing to tune in to only one or two stations may be comfortable, but it is not transformative. The voices we want to hear are not always the same as the voices we need to hear.

OPEN AND CLOSED DOORS

The book of Revelation picks up the language of the sower parable, repeating Jesus' refrain "Let those with ears to hear listen!" In a message to the church of Laodicea, Jesus declares, "Listen! I am standing at the door, knocking; if you hear my voice and open the door, I will come in to you and eat with you" (Revelation 3:20). The true listeners hear his voice and invite him in.

This text gives us another image to work with: listening as hospitality. In listening we open the door and receive a guest. When we listen we welcome others into our space. We open ourselves. When we listen, we invite others into places of vulnerability and potential intimacy. If we do it right, we won't fully know what we are getting ourselves into; we don't know who will come in and what they will bring with them. We are opening ourselves to surprise, to receiving strangers, to hearing the unexpected. We are opening ourselves to being changed. Jesus said he would come in and eat with those who hear his voice, and in his culture eating was an intimate act, something shared with people on your same social plane. Eating, and listening, level the playing field.

Revelation provides us a picture of listening that involves opening the door and letting another in. But if we're honest with ourselves, many times we keep the doors closed. Here are a few reasons why.

We're filled with noise. Life in this world sometimes has the feel of an emergency response scene: a cacophony of blaring sirens, screams, barking dogs and crisscrossed messages. It seems like there is no escape from noise. A writer for *The New Atlantis* called the relentless stimulation we encounter through our personal technology—emails, texts, videos, podcasts—"the great electronic din."[8] It's like eating every meal in a loud, packed restaurant. We are tempted to close our ears just to protect ourselves. Yet the noise creeps in, making it exceptionally difficult to create the internal quiet necessary for true listening.

Many of us lament how difficult it is to find stillness and to carve out calm amid the chaos. But the absence of quiet may actually reveal a resistance to quiet. Are we afraid of the voices in our heads that might start speaking if we took the time to be silent? Would we be turning up the volume on our fears, regrets and insecurities? We may subconsciously choose to be immersed in outer noise because it is more comfortable than facing the internal chatter.

We're lonely. Mother Teresa called loneliness the leprosy of the Western world, maybe even more devastating than Calcutta poverty.[9] Loneliness drives us to talk about ourselves to excess and to turn conversations toward ourselves. It makes us grasp on to others, thinking their role is to meet our needs, and it shrinks the space we have in our souls for welcoming others in. That loneliness would keep us from listening, and others from listening to us, is a tragedy, because being listened to is one of the great assurances in this universe that we are not alone.

We're afraid to change. To listen is to be to open change. If you enter a conversation without any possibility of having your mind changed, then you won't truly listen. Another way of putting this is that fear keeps us from listening. I know my own tendency to cling to beliefs and coping mechanisms because I fear the instability and uncertainty that will result if I release my grasp. But if we are truly prepared to listen, we have to be open to the possibility that some of our choices and beliefs limit us. We have to be open to admitting that we are wrong.

We're fragmented. True listening requires attention, an offering of ourselves for a period of time. We can be physically present with another person while our minds and hearts are far away. We may have internalized the cultural lie that our value is wrapped up in how busy we are. The more we do, the more we are in motion, the more significant we are. Further, our inner worlds so easily echo the pace and frenzy of our outer worlds, and we are busy and scattered, constantly multitasking but doing nothing particularly well, including listening.

TECHNOLOGY AND THE EROSION OF LISTENING

It seems that if you want to be a spiritual writer these days, you have to include at least a small rant about the way technology is ruining everything we hold dear. The Roman Empire fell when the Visigoths invaded from the north, and our modern Western civilization began to fall when Steve Jobs introduced the iPhone. But I don't believe that in order to be spiritually mature we have to eschew technology, write letters by hand and take long, daily walks into the woods. After all, I recently did a Skype chat with some family members where I held my cat up to the screen so they could say hi to her. I never want to again live in a world where that isn't a thing.

I do believe that genuine, if incomplete, connection is possible through mediating technology, and many people who I originally met online have now become good friends. Further, there are phenomenal online tools for deepening your spirituality and connecting to ancient church traditions.

That being said, I'm convinced that life in our wired society is contributing to the erosion of our capacity for listening. For all the doors that our personal technology opens for us, it is closing other doors, one of which is our ability to listen. Some of this is obvious. The best kind of listening involves not only our sense of hearing but all our senses, and if our eyes are focused on a screen and our fingers are sending texts, then we're not able to fully listen to the person right next to us.

What is less obvious is how the Internet, smartphones and social media are changing the physical characteristics of our brains by rerouting our neural pathways. We like to think that we are the ones acting on our devices, but the truth is that our devices also act on us. Many neurological studies demonstrate that our technology is reshaping our brains so that it not only seems more difficult to concentrate on one thing, it *is* harder to concentrate on one thing. If we're immersed in technology day after day, our brains are automatically branching out to do several tasks at once, making it dif-

ficult to focus our attention on any one thing. Technology writer
Linda Stone says that our brains seem stuck in "continuous partial
attention."[10] In other words, we are actually taking on the characteristics of our technology, our brains echoing the patterns of
social media. Our brains buzz with tweets and sound bites and
rapid-fire video, popping with short bursts of disparate information, leaving us at times close to circuit overload. Our technology is producing a splintering effect in us and stripping us of
the ability to be fully present.

I've heard people say that as our access to information expands,
we are becoming exponentially more knowledgeable as a society
but no wiser. The seemingly infinite sources of information, and
the content they spit at us, have us sampling everything but digesting little. We also have the ability to create playlists of voices
that only say what we want to hear and filter out voices that challenge us to think differently. If we don't like what our pastor
preaches in church, we can find a podcast that will preach the
sermon we want to hear. Wisdom, on the other hand, is a deep,
relational knowledge that comes through slow listening, allowing
what we hear to steep and simmer in us. And it requires us to listen
to voices that challenge us and present us with the unexpected,
forcing us to weigh what we hear against what we believe.

One last concern I have about our personal technology is what
it is teaching us about listening itself. A former college ministry
colleague once reported this scene to me: as he walked through
campus he passed hundreds of students, some walking in groups,
others walking alone, and he estimated that 60 percent of them,
including those walking in groups, were wearing earbuds. I fear
that our technology too often communicates that listening is an
action that *closes* us. They may help us attune to our inner worlds
at times, but headphones have become a symbol for expressing just

how selective and individualistic our listening can be. We are on the wrong track if the way we listen encases and shelters us. My hope is that we will treat listening as an act of hospitality, one that opens us to the world, to the people in front of us and to the Lord who knocks at the door.

DIGITAL VERSUS ANALOG LISTENING

Last year I joined the growing ranks of people who have made the return to music on vinyl. There is much debate in my family as to whether I'm a hipster or will soon be eating dinner at 4 p.m. and wearing chest-high pants. I have been persuaded that the analog sound imprinted on records makes a "warmer" sound, which may be the result of a bass sound that is less accurate than what is recorded on digital music files. Vinyl simply sounds more real, more alive, more human to me than some flat, very precise digital recordings.

What took some adjustment was how often you have to flip a record to the other side. The technical name for a record is LP, which stands for "long play," and I can only think of someone saying that sarcastically, because each side is about twenty minutes long. I was accustomed to a nonstop music stream of looping playlists and Internet radio. At first, I found the brevity of a record annoying, but then I realized I needed to change the way I listen to music. Now, after I get home from work I put on a record, put my feet up, close my eyes and listen to one side of an album from beginning to end.

The nature of the older technology requires me to make listening the center of my attention for extended periods of time. It's too distracting to listen to vinyl while I'm doing other things, because of how often I have to flip the record. When I listen to a record, it gets my focus.

How we listen to music in our digital age often reflects the way we listen in general. Music plays on a loop in the background, as a companion to whatever else we are doing. It is a soundtrack that goes with us, maybe augmenting our lives but not usually the centerpiece of our attention; sometimes it is simply white noise. Similarly, listening, for us, is an accompaniment to whatever else has our focus at the time. Other people often get our partial attention, and we listen to them from the side of our lives.

Listening to music on vinyl has taught me to put listening, in all spheres of life, at the center of my attention. It doesn't mean that I'm always listening; rather it means that when I do listen I give it my focus. I stop whatever else I am doing, sit down and set my energy toward whoever is speaking for a period of time. That devoted time of listening is more valuable than hours of partial listening. It is the difference between hearing music on an elevator while you ride to your floor and sitting in a concert hall and listening to a world-class symphony.

I SEE YOU

Even with the ubiquity of music, we live in a culture where the visual is king. Pixels are our currency, and video, icons and images are our shared language. Nike and Apple no longer need words to explain themselves; the swoosh and the partially eaten apple are more than sufficient.[11] Even in our spoken language, we employ a surprising number of words that derive from the sense of sight. If you spend much time in boardrooms, church-planting meetings or leadership circles you will hear words like *vision, focus, big picture, big idea, clarity* and *insight*, which all contain the sense or act of seeing. Seeing is all the buzz.

We associate the eyes with identity: they are the windows of the soul. And we associate them with intimacy: eye contact is one of the most powerful displays of intimacy. When we are feeling vulnerable before another person, we say they are peering directly into us or burning holes into us with their eyes. No one writes love songs about getting lost in your ears.

The relationship between sight and personal knowledge is an ancient equation. In classical Greek the word for "to see" literally means "to know." The philosopher Heraclitus claimed that "eyes are more accurate witnesses than ears," and Aristotle declared, "Above all we value sight . . . because sight is the principle source of knowledge."[12] Philosophy professor Don Ihde observes that there is a high degree of "intimacy between vision and the ultimately real for Greek thought."[13]

I find this connection between vision, knowledge and the nature of reality a little surprising because what is seen—the world outside of us—can by itself tell us very little about how to interpret it. We begin to make sense of things, and probe deeper into them, through hearing, language, and conversation and instruction.

Metaphors for sight alone are insufficient to represent personal identity and knowledge. Walter Ong points out that the sense of sight, in contrast to hearing, takes things apart: "Vision comes to a human being one direction at a time; to look at a room or landscape, I must move my eyes around from one part to another."[14] My power to look at one thing rather than another makes sight highly controllable, and it emphasizes the distance between me and the object I am looking at. In contrast, sound incorporates and unifies. Acoustic space is less controllable than visual space. Sound surrounds us, immersing us in it, and even pours into us.[15] The physiology of the ear dictates that sound must penetrate, entering into the recesses of our skull. Sound breaks down the hard distinction between subject and object, and through listening we participate in the minds and lives of others.

THE PRIORITY OF LISTENING

We may say that "seeing is believing," but in the Bible, for the most part, *hearing* is believing. The spectacle of the burning bush may have drawn Moses to the spot, but he didn't know he was on sacred ground until the voice commanded him to take off his shoes. Seeing God, in fact, can be quite hazardous to your health. The sense of sight is even linked in some cases with idolatry. When Moses retells the exodus story for a new generation, he repeatedly warns them about creating forms to represent God. He reminds them that "the LORD spoke to you out of the fire. You heard the sound of words but saw no form; there was only a voice" (Deuteronomy 4:12). God is invisible, and though God sometimes displays himself in the visual, his persistent means of communication with his people throughout history is speech, in one form or another. We receive his revelations to us through obedient listening.

The priority of listening in the Scriptures is well established. But what is unexpected is that the God who spoke the world and the Bible into existence is *also* a listener.

TWO

The King Who Listens

THE KINGS OF HISTORY ARE REWARDED with many impressive descriptors: *majestic, exalted, glorious, sovereign*. Men and women bow before such heights of nobility; even the eyes of wealth and status fall to the ground as the king passes. When his majesty makes a proclamation, the trumpets sound, the royal standard is raised and the people kneel with a hush.

I suspect that few kings have been lauded for their ability and willingness to listen. We don't have to dig deep into the annals of royal history to find kings who had finely tuned senses yet were strangely deaf. Henry VIII rejected the pope's authority in his personal life and divided the church. Napolean ignored his advisors who opposed an invasion of Russia and found himself in island exile. King George III and Parliament refused to heed the growing unrest of the colonies against taxation and incited war. If Saruman had listened to Gandalf he wouldn't have been stuck in a cold tower with Wormtongue. The pages of the Bible are stained with the blood of kings who would not listen to God or their counselors, revealing the perilous temptation of all human kings, and probably all human beings, to usurp divine prerogative. Shakespeare would lead us to believe that the machinations required for gaining absolute power have a way of rupturing the eardrums, so that all kings can hear in the end is the sound of their own voices. After all, if megalomaniacs were able to listen, they wouldn't be megalomaniacs.

It seems that the more power you have in the human kingdom, the less you feel obligated to listen. There are exceptions, of course. Winston Churchill said that "courage is what it takes to stand up and speak; courage is also what it takes to sit down and listen." Yet historical evidence too often indicates that throne rooms are soundproof. Once you have settled into the plushest seat in the land you can surround yourself with sycophants who have one line on their job descriptions: do your majesty's bidding. They have to listen to you; you are required to listen to no one. Power and listening in the human realm usually have a zero-sum gain; the more a person ascends the ladder, the harder it is to hear what's happening down below. Power is an incredibly effective earplug. There is a reason why the phrase "speak truth to power" exists; power generally doesn't listen well.

It should come as no surprise when God, the heavenly King, exercises his sovereign right to speak. If anyone is entitled to issue proclamations on any subject he desires, amid all the fanfare the nations can muster, it is the Lord Almighty. The true King has spoken the prime word, from which all words trace their source, and he will have the last word, when all words will fall silent at his feet. But what might blindside us is the discovery that the God of the Bible listens. The cosmos hangs together by his word, galaxies and constellations obey when he speaks, but the undisputed champion of creation is a listener. God has absolutely no obligation to pay attention to anyone or anything. He could wield his power however he chooses and everyone could only clear out of the way. The Lord astonishes us and completely flips power on its ear by entering into listening relationships with people. In no other royal court have hearings been so generously extended.

There is a scandalous little line that occurs twice in the New King James Version of the Psalms, when the praying person entreats God to "bow down Your ear" (Psalm 31:2; 86:1). Consider the implications of such an invocation. A subject of the Most High, who ought to approach in trembling obeisance, asks the King *to bow down to him.* We picture the master stooping to the level of the servant, bending his neck so the servant can speak at his eye level, the King's ear to the subject's mouth. Our surprise grows when we recall that an act of listening is an act of obedience, and it turns out that "bow down Your ear" perfectly captures what is required for the Lord to listen to humans. It's what theologians of previous generations used to call the "condescension" of the Lord, but they didn't mean it with the negative connotations it carries today. The Lord lowers himself to pay attention to an individual's particular troubles, even doing for her what she asks. What kind of king is this who would kneel down before his subjects?

We find ourselves at the heart of the gospel mystery—that the heavenly King not only speaks but listens, that he not only commands obedience but obeys commands. God's serving nature does not make him servile to our desires; he does not serve out of slavish compulsion or hollow duty, but of a freely chosen posture of servanthood, because that is who he is.

This is no ordinary king. From the very beginning of the Scriptures we find a God who does not hoard power but shares it. Created in God's image, humans are given the kingly responsibility of co-ruling creation, subduing it and representing the Lord to it. Psalm 8 builds on the vice regency bestowed on human beings:

> You have made them a little lower than God,
>   and crowned them with glory and honor.

You have given them dominion over the works of your
    hands;
  you have put all things under their feet. (vv. 5-6)

Much later the risen and exalted Jesus gives his followers a great
commission to act and speak on his behalf. The power of his reign,
available through the Holy Spirit, would be present to them as they
carried out his mission. The apostle Paul promised Timothy that
those who endure will reign with Christ, and Revelation echoes
that the saints redeemed from every tribe will reign on earth when
the kingdom comes.

The God who shares power is a listener. Listening is not something that becomes necessary for God only after the world is
created. Listening is who God is. In God's very being, communication does not move unilaterally but flows back and forth and
around the three persons of the Trinity—Father, Son, Holy Spirit.
The triune nature of God puts listening right at the center of the
universe. God is love, and love requires listening. The inner
workings of the divine life are held together by a self-giving, recip-
rocating and listening nature, so when Son is revealed in human
form he says he does not do what he wants but what his Father
commands, and when the Spirit comes it guides people into all
truth because it only speaks what it hears. In the work of creation,
redemption and mission the persons of the Trinity reveal the listening that has been at the heart of their relationships all along.

The paradox of the King who listens comes to its climax in the
Messiah. The New Testament gives us an astonishing picture of
kingship: the true king is not the one who wields his power but the
one who surrenders his power and serves. It would seem that the
ruler who jealously guards his power is in fact a ruler with insufficient power. Jesus abdicated his heavenly throne, emptying

himself of power and privilege, in order to become a servant. That is why listening is so central to the gospel: it is the indispensable attribute of a servant. Emptying yourself, assuming the role of a servant and submitting to others is not only the description of Christ's incarnation, it is also the description of a true listener.

Jesus came not to be served but to serve. He came not to be heard but to hear. He shrank so that others might have room, and he bent down his ear so that the unheard voices would be honored. In doing so, he utterly redefined what kingship is. Here is a king who serves his subjects, washes their feet and listens for their needs beyond even what they know they need. Here is a king who does not ask his people to die for him but who instead dies for them. The servant heart that led him to listen to others is the same heart that led him to the cross.

THE REAL KING LISTENS

The Scriptures may be God's Word spoken to us, but the Bible would be a really short book if God wasn't also a listener. If the King didn't listen, later generations would not have received anything beyond the book of Genesis, and more likely there wouldn't have been any future generations of faith at all. The Hebrew slaves we meet in Exodus would have been left to languish, making bricks to the glory of Pharaoh. Fortunately for them, and for us, the Bible narrates not only God's speech but also his acts of listening.

The rescue of the Hebrew people from their Egyptian captors, their central national memory, did not begin with a hasty exit out of the land. It did not begin with the Passover meal, nor did it commence when Moses and Aaron crossed the threshold into Pharaoh's chamber and demanded that he let the people go. It did not even begin when a bush flared up and started talking in the Midian desert. The exodus began when God *heard*. "The Israelites groaned under their slavery, and cried out. Out of the slavery their cry for help rose up to God. *God heard their groaning*, and God remembered his covenant with Abraham, Isaac, and Jacob" (Exodus 2:23-24, italics added). Just as the Lord heard Abel's shed blood crying out from the ground generations before, he heard the misery of his people crushed by oppression. An act of listening started the wheels of redemptive history turning.

On that day the battle begins between the King of Israel and the king of Egypt, and the confrontation reveals not only who is the supreme power but who is the greater listener. It is a grand listening contest played out on a historical stage. In contrast to the Lord who hears the groans of his people, Pharaoh is introduced as one who absolutely refuses to listen. Again and again we read descriptions like this: "Still Pharaoh's heart was hardened, and he would not listen to them" (Exodus 7:13). He would not hear the cries of the slaves, he would not heed the voice of their God and he wouldn't even listen to the agony of his people crushed under horrific plagues. On a deep level, the exodus story is a conversation about the character of true kingship and the nature of power. The pretender asserts his power through oppression and authoritarian rule, but the true King is moved by the cries of those in need. The crown belongs to the King who listens. And God has never stopped listening to the groans of slaves.

SURPRISED BY LISTENING

I didn't get serious about listening until people who I didn't expect to listen to me did. My understanding of listening up until that point was largely positional, meaning that you listen when you are in particular positions or roles. I thought it was the responsibility of employees to listen to bosses, children to listen to parents, interns to listen to mentors. Teachers give lectures, superiors tell you what to do, pastors preach and everyone else listens. You listen mostly by default.

I expected more of the same when I began a chaplain internship, a rigorous, self-reflective and sometimes painful requirement for ordination. For four months I served as an intern at St. Joseph's Hospital in Orange, California, working with patients on the cancer floor. Most patients were either in chemotherapy or suffering from advanced stages of cancer, and too often I watched them fade from vitality and hope to despair and lifelessness. Mostly I sat and listened, because I had no idea what else to do. One day I sat outside the room of a patient dying of breast cancer as her family—her parents, her sister, her six-year-old son, her three-year-old daughter and her utterly lost husband—went in, one by one, to say goodbye. Another afternoon I listened to the confession of a homeless man oppressed by chemotherapy and a life full of regrets.

Donna was my supervisor, and when she and I met individually in the first week, I braced myself for the standard instruction, correction and advice. But that day I encountered a different kind of leadership: I met an authority figure who listened to me. Donna was interested in *me*, not in telling me what to do or shaping me in her image. She asked me what I thought and felt, what I cared about, what my family was like, who I wanted to be. She listened to me so intently that I would get uncomfortable talking about myself for so long. I would try to turn the conversation toward her, but she knew to redirect it back to me.

As Donna and I continued to meet that fall, I began to realize that I wasn't her project. She wasn't looking for what she needed to fix about me. The more she listened to me, the more I began to see myself the way she did: as a person. I wasn't a sick patient, which is the message I had received from previous mentors who seemed intent on performing emergency surgery on my soul. I had been told a thousand times that God loved me. I don't remember whether Donna ever said that during our weekly meetings, but I completed that internship knowing God's love in ways I never had before. I began to feel a new kind of peace within myself, and I was filled with a new level of energy for ministry, one that was not motivated by emptiness but by fullness because I had received one of God's greatest gifts: the gift of being truly heard.

Over the past few years, I have asked many people this question: has there ever been a person in your life who surprised you with listening? They usually have to think for a while, which probably indicates how rarely we are truly heard. But then they remember, and they tell a story about an authority figure—a parent, a teacher, a pastor, a boss—who listened to them unexpectedly and how it changed them. I have had enough of these conversations now that I can say that all the lectures and sermons we hear, all the books we read, all the instruction and advice we receive do not compare to the transformative power of being heard.

Donna, and other listeners like her, can listen to others because they have met a God who listens. I realized during that internship that Donna's God was much less preachy and pedantic than mine, and far more welcoming. When she read Psalm 139, it was comforting to her that there was nowhere to flee from God's presence, whereas, if I'm honest, I found it terrifying. When my God listened, it was with a glass-to-the-door, eavesdropping for me to say the wrong thing, ready to play "gotcha!" with the mistakes I made. Donna taught me that when we encounter a God who listens, who welcomes us into his space, it changes both how we view God and how we view ourselves.

THE BEGINNING OF LISTENING

Listening begins when we learn that our heavenly Father listens to us. The pattern of human life may be that we listen first, but with the Lord, we are always heard before we hear. God does not listen partially or dismissively. His listening is not a stall, designed to humor us until we tire ourselves out. Our King gives us his attention, turning his face toward us, a servant ready to ask, "What do you want me to do for you?" (Matthew 20:32).

In the Scriptures God's listening and God's acting are often treated synonymously. God is moved inwardly by prayer, and his outward responses are so intertwined with his listening that they can be spoken of interchangeably. Here is the true active listener; he acts on what he hears. The common complaint that someone is "hearing but not listening" does not apply to God. It is a human shortcoming to receive words into our ear canals but not let them move us any further. Perhaps the process of transformation into God's image involves a gradual narrowing of the divide between hearing and acting.

This disconnect does not exist with God. I know of no place in the Scriptures where a person says that God *heard* my prayer and does not at least imply that God *acted* on my prayer. On many occasions biblical authors use the phrase "God heard" when we might think instead to say "God answered." We would employ a metaphor for speech—*answer*—when biblical writers use a listening metaphor to indicate that God responded.

Eighteenth-century American theologian Jonathan Edwards, in a sermon called "The Prayer-Hearing God," said that what distinguishes the true God from the false gods is that the true God *hears prayer*. The gods that the ancient nations prayed to "cannot hear, and cannot answer their prayer." But, "it is the character of the Most High, that he is a God who hears prayer."[1] Every time someone whispers a prayer or simply looks heavenward, they cling to the hope that God is a listener. The "power of prayer" is located precisely in the One who has prayer-hearing power. Edwards elaborates on what he means by God hearing prayer: (1) God *accepts* the supplications of those who pray to him, and (2) God *acts* in accordance with his acceptance of their prayers. Enfolded in God's listening is his accepting of prayer and his acting on it.

The Hebrew writers of the Old Testament commonly employ a rhetorical device called parallelism, in which they emphasize a point by repeating it in the next line but with different words. For example, the Psalms regularly replace *hear* or *listen* with a verb we would consider more active, like *save*, and vice versa. Psalm 55 is a prominent example:

> But I call upon God,
>> and the LORD will save me.
> Evening and morning and at noon
>> I utter my complaint and moan,
>> and he will hear my voice.
> He will redeem me unharmed
>> from the battle that I wage,
>> for many are arrayed against me.
> God, who is enthroned from of old,
>> will hear, and will humble them. (Psalm 55:16-19)

The writer replaces "save" in the first verse with "hear my voice" in the second, then returns to "redeem me unharmed," moves back to "will hear" and then summarizes it all with "will hear, and will humble them." The psalmist can comfortably toggle between verbs for hearing and verbs for acting because they are so conflated in the nature of God. There are times in the Scriptures when writers do delineate between God's hearing and acting, but even in those instances there are no sharp lines drawn. Biblical listening has evidence, or better, acting is the completion of the listening process. If listening is the inhale, then acting is the exhale, and without the entire system there is no life.

GOD QUESTIONS

In the Bible we meet a God who asks questions. Sometimes his questions are rhetorical, but usually they have a genuine, curious and open-ended tone. I believe a key difference between God's voice and the sinister voices we sometimes encounter is how they ask questions. The first time we encounter evil in the Scriptures, the serpent asks the woman a question: "Did God say, 'You shall not eat from any tree in the garden'?" (Genesis 3:1). The serpent slithers around the truth, distorting God's invitation to "freely eat of every tree of the garden; *but* of the tree of the knowledge of good and evil you shall not eat" (Genesis 2:16-17, italics added). The tempter counters God's gift with a leading and insidious question meant to spark mistrust and inhibit relationship.

Compare that to the question God asks at his next entrance: "Where are you?" I once pictured that scene as God hunting down his ungrateful children, his question intended to draw them out of their hiding place so he could take them down. Instead I have come to hear his question as an invitation, an extension of relationship even after his creatures have scorned relationship. Presumably God knows where they are, yet he gives them an opportunity to respond and to rejoin the conversation with him. The tempter asked questions to divide and provoke, but God asks questions to elicit dialogue, a true give-and-take, and he is genuinely, even astonishingly, interested in our responses.

Jesus posed questions that invited genuine and open dialogue, especially when he encountered true seekers. In a turning point in Mark's Gospel, Jesus put the decisive question to his disciples:

"Who do you say that I am?" He didn't grab Peter by the tunic and yell, "I'm the Messiah, you rube!" He was not afraid of asking the hard questions because he wanted people to arrive at their own conclusions.

Sometimes Jesus asks questions playfully. At the end of Luke's Gospel, he joins two disillusioned followers on their sad walk back from Jerusalem. They thought they had found the Messiah, but his life ended in crucified silence. A stranger intercepts them, a slight sparkle in his eyes, and asks, "What are you discussing with each other while you walk along?" They are incredulous: Have you been in a cave, man? Are you the only one who doesn't know the things that have happened? The stranger shrugs. "What things?" [*wink*]. There is humor and joy in this interaction, but Jesus is patient and doesn't spoil the surprise, because he doesn't want to drop the truth on them. He gives them space to express their disappointment and the tension they are feeling. This is one of the greatest challenges for a listener: to delay your response so that others can express their present emotions and unresolved tensions. In asking questions and holding back his answers, Jesus invites honesty, vulnerability and intimacy. Plus, he seems to enjoy it.

Sometimes God's listening abilities are so profound as to become doctrinally problematic. Think of Abraham and his bartering with the Lord over the fate of Sodom, in which he somehow manages to whittle down God's wrath on the people of the city. Or consider Moses persuading God to change his mind and to keep his promise after the nation of Israel's apostasy with the golden calf. These stories have had theologians turning interpretive somersaults for generations. Whatever we make of the anthropomorphic pictures of God changing his mind and making compromises, we have to conclude that God is an extravagant listener, deeply moved by the appeals of his people.

THE JESUS SCHOOL OF LISTENING

The church throughout the ages has been eager to speak like Jesus. It makes sense, since he drew a crowd wherever he taught. His words, encased in red letters in our Bibles, are spirit and life, bestowing forgiveness, healing the sick and resurrecting the dead. Jesus embodies the Father's speech to us, but he also represents the Father's willingness to listen to us. He is not only God's predestined spokesman, he is also God's appointed listener. In order for the King to announce the good news into the world, he must first hear the bad news of the world's brokenness and enslavement. So in order to fully imitate him, we must matriculate in the Jesus school of listening.

Wide. Jesus listened widely. Perhaps most striking is not *how* he listened but *who* he listened to. Jesus had a habit of listening to the people that others ignored—the poor, the sick, the pariahs, the foreigners, the sinners. Many of the powerful in his society seemed unable to hear the cries of these people, as though they were out of earshot. But Jesus' hearing was finely tuned to the voices of those who seemed farthest away. He would turn a deaf ear on those who thought they had a right to be heard, but he would drop everything to listen to the smallest voice.

When Bartimaeus, the blind man of Jericho, screamed for help, the crowds tried to shush him. But Jesus, the Gospel writer Mark tells us, "stood still." Perhaps standing still is the beginning of listening. The residents of Jericho quickened their pace when they were close to the blind man, but Jesus, his path laid out before him to Jerusalem, stopped. He then asked Bartimaeus, "What do you want me to do for you?" (Mark 10:51). Has the world ever known a more beautiful question? This is the question of a servant. It is the question that Jesus puts to all who long for healing, and he listens for our response.

Deep. Jesus' listening also went deep. It had a probing, penetrating quality to it, able to hear what's unsaid. Jesus had Jedi listening skills. One of his favorite techniques for digging beneath the surface was answering a question with a question. It is an incredibly effective, if not somewhat maddening, technique for locating a person's motivations. A teacher of the law inquires, "Teacher, what must I do to inherit eternal life?" and Jesus replies, "What is the written in the law? What do you read there?" Jesus breaks the lawyer's serve by returning his question with another question, and in doing so forces the lawyer to reveal his intentions. The man was not seeking answers as much as he was seeking to be impressive.

In his listening Jesus also has an acute ability to detect underlying needs. He is rarely convinced by the religious presentations that people give him but insists on probing to the deeper levels of a person's true desires. When Jesus meets the Samaritan woman at Jacob's well in John 4, there are two conversations that take place simultaneously: the Samaritan's surface reading of their interaction and Jesus' deeper listening.

I once heard renowned preacher Brenda Salter McNeil call the Samaritan woman "Sam," and now when I read that story I can't think of her in any other way. Sam labors to keep the conversation with Jesus on the literal level. She is determined to keep her interaction with this strange Jewish man focused on drinking water, buckets and hills. Jesus, on the other hand, listens for the inner stirrings underneath her routines and checkered past, the emotions and fears that sound below the words. He is able to hear the shame and rejection that require Sam to draw water alone in the heat of the day. He listens to the deep longings and subterranean disappointments that have accompanied her through so many broken relationships. His listening dares to mine unexplored places.

For a long time I assumed the setting of the well was incidental to the story, or perhaps a symbol of Jesus' primacy over the patriarch Jacob who planted the well. But what if the well, plunging to unknown depths, is another character, representing the conversation that is happening beneath the surface? It reflects the story underneath the story, representing the cavernous needs and longings in Sam's life. Sam keeps the conversation to the shallow container on the surface, but Jesus listens into the hidden places sunk in her soul and brings her secret pain to the surface. The water that he promises her will spring up in those deep and wounded places into everlasting life, drawing her out of her dark well into the light.

Presence. Throughout his ministry, Jesus demonstrates that true listening is a profound act of hospitality. Proximity is critical to how he listens. He invites people into his presence, bringing them front and center, which is especially powerful for those who reside on the margins of society. Every time he welcomes a tax collector or prostitute into his space, he redraws the cultural and religious map. The outcast is brought to the center, and the arrogant religious authority is pushed to the periphery. He changes the social status of the ignored just by listening to their voices.

In Jesus we meet a listener who gives his full attention to people. He never listens with just one ear. When a stranger from the crowd touched his garment, he was not content to have his healing power work its magic and go on his way; he insisted on meeting the woman who touched him. He wanted to hear her whole story, not so he would feel informed but so she would feel known. When a rich man approached Jesus and asked how he could inherit eternal life, Jesus did not wave him off with a quick piece of advice. He received him and loved him. He was moved. He listened with his whole self.

I spent the first five years of ministry trying to talk like Jesus. I blasted out of seminary with a "teaching gift" and landed directly behind the pulpit in my first job. I stood up in front of people every Sunday, and I talked real good. I have spent the last five years trying to listen like Jesus, a process that has taken much greater effort. I began by noticing how he listens to me, and it has only made me love him more. A Lord who speaks truth to me is good and right; a Lord who listens to me is grace and mystery and glory. As I have committed to listening like Jesus, I have found myself even more immersed in his work. And somehow, I am finding that I now talk a lot more like he does too.

WHEN GOD DOESN'T LISTEN

The union of hearing and acting in God's character is at once comforting and, if we're honest, troubling, because it raises the question, What about when God is silent?

No one is immune to this conflict; Mother Teresa was plagued by it all her life.[2] The interrelatedness of God's hearing and acting frames the question in a freshly disturbing way: If God is not acting on my prayer, does that mean he is not listening to me? Worse, does that mean I have some block that is muzzling God's work in my life? Is our conversation broken because of something in me?

It is a common saying in church circles that God hears all prayers, but biblically speaking, it is hard to support. There are clear examples of the Lord turning a deaf ear:

- "Take away from me the noise of your songs; I *will not listen to the melody of your harps*. But let justice roll down like waters, and righteousness like an ever-flowing stream" (Amos 5:23-24, italics added).

- "The Lord's hand is not too short to save, nor his ear too dull to hear. Rather, your iniquities have been barriers between you and your God, and *your sins have hidden his face from you so that he does not hear*" (Isaiah 59:1-2, italics added).

- "When one will not listen to the law, even one's prayers are an abomination" (Proverbs 28:9).

- "And whenever you pray, do not be like the hypocrites; for they love to stand and pray in the synagogues and at the street corners, so that they may be seen by others. Truly I tell you, they have received their reward. But whenever you pray, go into your room and shut the door and pray to your Father who is in secret; and your Father who sees in secret will reward you. When you are praying, do not heap up empty phrases as the Gentiles do; for they think that they will be heard because of their many words. Do not be like them, for your Father knows what you need before you ask him" (Matthew 6:5-8).

- "We know that God does not listen to sinners, but he does listen to one who worships him and obeys his will" (John 9:31).

The people who the God of the Old Testament hears are the same people who his Son has a hearing preference for in the New: the contrite, the humble, the poor, the sincere. But the prayers of oppressors, the unjust, the unrepentant, the self-righteous and the violent do not cross the threshold of God's throne room. When the band strikes up the tune of insincerity and injustice, the Lord will not dance. It seems that God's ear is inclined toward those who themselves are listeners. When people abuse their power, they have shown themselves unwilling to listen—both to the correction of the Lord and to the cries of others—and God will not listen to them. It is the penitent tax collector, not the self-important Pharisee, whose prayers are heard.

This is where the gift of confession enters the conversation.

There may be times when unconfessed sins interrupt the listening conversation between us and God, and we usually know when this happens because every time we try to pray, the sin comes to mind. Sometimes we will be called to confess and reconcile to another person before we come before God, and at other times we will need to forgive the debts of others in order to fully embrace that our debts have been forgiven. The good news is that we can trust that God's ears are always open to repentance.

THE DARK NIGHT

If only it were always that simple though. Part of me wishes that we could always reduce those seasons when God does not seem to listen to unacknowledged sin. But that does not do justice to the experiences of saints who have gone before us, those who have agonized over God's apparent absence while remaining unwaveringly faithful to him.

Prayer is not a ladder we build to the heavens; rather, as Dietrich Bonhoeffer put it, prayer is God's work in us. When we do not turn away from God in times of distress or confusion, I believe it is also an indication that God has not turned away from us. When a person prays or just looks longingly in a heavenward direction, even though she may feel abandoned, her prayer is an indication of God's ongoing presence.

Many spiritual sages would remind us not to mistake the *experience* of God's presence for the presence itself. We have consistent biblical pictures of a God who pursues his children to the ends of the earth, whose ears are open to them, who loves them as passionately and protectively as parents love their children. He is Immanuel, God with us, until the end of the age.

Although we are tempted in times of agonizing silence to think of God with an icy stare on his face, refusing to make eye contact,

I have found it comforting to think of God simply sitting with us in our pain, quietly listening. Maybe what feels like awkward and anxious silences to us are actually full and gentle silences. We are reminded that listening is not inaction. When God is listening to us, even if we do not experience the results we hope for, he is actively disposed toward us. We must also remember that the fact that God hears prayers does not make him servile to our demands. Prayer words are not incantations with innate power to change divine weather patterns. When God doesn't give us our specific prayer requests, it may be an indication that he is working different things into us: things like trust, dependence, humility, patience, wisdom, even intimacy with him.

I find that I have an impossible time trying to get God to share the urgency that I feel about certain things. As much as I would like him to chase my ambulances all around the city, the Lord just does not seem as preoccupied or anxious about my life circumstances as I am. It's maddening. Sometimes it even seems like God's silences have a message in them: *Slow down.* That's why I have learned over the years to listen for the silences as much as I listen for the voices, because there are hints in those silences. It's not unlike what my friends do with a hyperactive child. Instead of scolding or forcing him to sit down, they just let the kid wear himself out. He yells and jumps and spins around—within the boundaries they have set—until eventually the sugar wears off and he collapses. I have a suspicion that sometimes God goes silent to let me wear myself out with all my frustrations and shouts of unfairness and carefully worded arguments that mostly mask temper-tantrums, until I am exhausted and perhaps ready to finally listen.

There is an experience common to all Christians, articulated best by St. John of the Cross, a sixteenth-century mystic, called the dark night of the soul. The idea is that in the beginning stages of faith,

God's voice booms in the life of the new believer. Prayer is electric, devotional reading is a feast for the soul, the spiritual life is a conveyor belt that does all the walking for us as we close in on the Lord. But at a certain point, someone turns off the lights. This stage is often called the dark night of the senses. The "sense" of God's presence has all but disappeared; our eyes don't see his glory, our ears don't hear his consolations, our hands don't touch his wounds. What was once a raging love affair becomes a lukewarm marriage, a couple sitting at a nice restaurant on their anniversary with nothing to say.

This is where St. John encourages us not to give up, because it's in this stage of the relationship when the hard work of love really begins. God withdraws a sense of his presence so that we do not seek the glamour and the intoxication of his glory but instead we would seek *him*. Even though we do not feel God's listening presence upon us, God is listening and silently working through our doubts and struggles. God may not be directly answering our prayers, but he is silently walking through our lives, beckoning us closer, working new things into us.

THREE

Listening to God

IT IS A TALE OF TWO MOUNTAINS. The prophet Elijah sweeps onto the scene halfway through the book of 1 Kings, confident and brazen, the word of the Lord on his lips. His obedience to God's commands, even when those instructions are weird and unappetizing, such as "eat what the ravens feed you," is impeccable. He listens to the Lord, and the Lord listens to him. He believes God's announcement that a famine will oppress Israel, and when he prays that the drought on the withered land would cease, the Lord obliges with an undersized but potent raincloud.

The first half of Elijah's story culminates on Mount Carmel, the high place the rebellious nation had devoted to the fertility god Baal. The bold prophet proposes a cosmic showdown between the deities and their respective worshipers. You make an altar to your so-called god, Elijah contends, and I'll make an altar to mine, and we'll see who speaks with flames. The one who rains down fire and consumes the sacrifice is the true God. Bring it on, prophets of Baal.

In a feature film, Mount Carmel would be captured with the wide-angle shot and the epic soundtrack, while Elijah struts around the pinnacle, mocking his enemies and calling down fire from heaven. The action would be shown in slow motion as the flames engulf the sacrifice and the battle of the prophets ensues,

Baal's followers fleeing for their lives. For Elijah, Mount Carmel is the peak of triumph, the climax of God's justice and truth, the height of his ministry, the adrenaline rush of his prophetic call.

One chapter later we find a very different Elijah on a new mountain, vulnerable, fragile, less superhero and more human. Even though he's perched on a mountain, it feels like a downslope, the degrading of his prophetic ministry. After the stir he created at Carmel, Jezebel, the wife of the king, has vowed to take our hero's life. Alone and shivering in a cave, he is emptied of his hubris and afraid for his life. In the cinematic retelling this scene gets a melancholy ballad and a zoom lens that captures his somber stares and despairing sighs.

This is no random peak in the desert. Elijah quivers on the same mountain that, centuries before, the newly liberated Hebrews had trembled before when the Lord wrote his law on stone tablets. Without prompting, the prophet has fled from the fangs of Jezebel to the face of Mount Horeb, known to previous generations as Mount Sinai. The narrative parallels are hard to miss. Elijah has trekked forty days and forty nights away from Israel back through the wilderness, reversing the paths that the Hebrew people walked for forty years before crossing the Jordan. He seems to want to go back in time, to an era when God's calling was clear, when the Israelites' vocation was in front of them and there was no question which God they worshiped.

In the first act on that mountain God had appeared in smoke, thunder and fire, and the people couldn't bear it. They begged their leader Moses to intercede for them, and he encountered God on the holy mountain. In one dramatic scene, God passed by Moses in all his fullness while hiding him in a mountaintop crevice, lest the mortal be consumed by glory. So, in act two, when the voice beckons Elijah out of his shelter and tells him to "stand on the mountain before the Lord, for the Lord is about to pass by," Elijah doesn't need to consult his Bible to understand what is happening. The Lord may be gracious and slow to anger, but this is still the sort of thing that can get a man vaporized. The next scene deserves to be quoted at length:

> Now there was a great wind, so strong that it was splitting mountains and breaking rocks in pieces before the LORD, but the LORD was not in the wind; and after the wind an earthquake, but the LORD was not in the earthquake; and after the earthquake a fire, but the LORD was not in the fire; and after the fire a sound of sheer silence. When Elijah heard it, he wrapped his face in his mantle and went out and stood at the entrance of the cave. Then there came a voice to him that said, "What are you doing here, Elijah?" (1 Kings 19:11-13)

The author of 1 Kings stirs up a potent cocktail of déjà vu. All the special effects of Sinai are revisited, brought before Elijah in a terrifying parade—the bitter wind, the rumbling quake, the conflagration—but this time, the Lord is not there. Ruth Haley Barton proposes that the turmoil happening outside the cave echoes the stirrings tormenting Elijah's inner world.[1] But then Elijah heard the silence—*he heard the silence*—and he knew it was the Lord. All the air was sucked out of the atmosphere, leaving nothing but Presence. This is no meek silence. This is a slap-you-in-the-face kind of silence.

The Lord moves Elijah from chaos to rest. It is the gift of the divine "stop!" While the imagery and language of the story derive from the exodus, one also catches hints of the creation story in the text. The primeval forces and basic elements are put to rest both in the atmosphere outside and in the climate of Elijah's life inside. God knew that in such a swirling chaos Elijah would be unlikely to hear his voice, and so he approaches the prophet in silence. Once silence has overtaken Elijah's soul, he is able to listen to God's voice. God's surprising work on Horeb does nothing to change Elijah's circumstances—he is still a wanted prophet hunted by a bloodthirsty queen—and yet somehow the interaction changes everything. The mount is transfigured from a place of despair and defeat to a place of courage and call re-created.

God speaks in the best of times and in the worst of times. He ascends to the heights with Elijah, shouting in a moment of triumph, and he descends to the depths, stilling his heart in a moment of despair. The Lord speaks in fire and the Lord speaks in silence; he thunders and he whispers. He asks questions and he makes proclamations, and whether in a hostile crowd or in isolation, the Voice sounds. The same God who speaks in activism and prophetic demonstration speaks in contemplation and solitude. Elijah lived in a "communicating cosmos,"[2] as Dallas Willard put it, and so do we. Our universe is piercingly personal because the God who stands over it and in it wants to communicate with us.

TOO PERSONAL

I am convinced that the scourge of our scientific and technological age is depersonalization. There is a heartbeat pulsating at the center of the universe, giving life and meaning to everything, but our need for control reduces everything to automation. When the life of the world loses its face and voice and ears, our worldviews become dependent on abstract cause and effect, set in motion by arbitrary, uncaring forces, and we seek to contain life in mechanical principles. We exploit the environment for our own ends without regard to consequences. We see people for what we can get out of them, how we can manipulate them to achieve our goals. We describe human beings like computers, with bytes and programs and bandwidth, or we find labels for them so that we can jam them into neat categories where they can't bother us. Our communication is mediated by screens, and too often we lead screen-sized lives, our quality time devoted to our personal technology. Morality becomes the dictate of tangible rules and formulaic answers, buttressed by a black and white world where I'm right and you're wrong. Religion becomes an intellectual assent to a doctrinal system rather than a wholehearted yes to a Person.

The message of Elijah's story, indeed of the whole sweep of the Bible, could not be more different from our impersonal cultural narrative. The biblical authors declare in one voice that we live in a universe with a face, a place of communion and conversation and intimacy. The depersonalized view is not actually progressive; it belongs to the idol worship of ancient nations. The prophet Jeremiah assured ancient Israel that "their idols are like scarecrows in a cucumber field, and they cannot speak; they have to be carried, for they cannot walk. Do not be afraid of them, for they cannot do evil, nor is it in them to do good" (Jeremiah 10:5). The idols could not be real because they were not personal, and the universe is governed by a Person who speaks and acts and moves.

Tim Keller has a theory that so many people reject Christianity because it is *too personal*. The transcendent power behind the universe has a personality and is capable of being, and wants to be, known. This power even has an appearance, shining in the face of Jesus Christ, and that level of personhood is too invasive for many people. We prefer our abstract, controllable images of deity that don't threaten us with the frightening prospect of real relationship.

FEAR IN HEARING

It is the nature of God to speak. If we're honest, this puts us in both a joyfully reassuring and utterly dangerous place. Somehow we find

ourselves both in the warmth of the womb and on the edge of a
cliff. To know that we are not alone, that the echoes of God's voice
resound to the ends of the earth, reminds us that the universe is a
perfectly safe place to be.[3] Loneliness loses some of its power when
we realize how truly "full" the universe is. The painful and thorny
questions, while not fading completely, have a way of melting away
before the presence of the Lord. At the same time, to affirm that
the true *God* speaks, not some divine projection of our imagination,
is terrifying, because *we have absolutely no control over what he will
say.* What if we don't like what we hear? To truly listen to such a
God will involve a radical openness to surprise, to risk, to change,
even to suffering. Or what if we don't like the timing of God's
speech? To truly listen will necessitate learning how to wait and to
trust, or even sometimes moving before we feel we're ready.

Perhaps the most common question asked about this subject is
"Why can't I hear God's voice?" but I wonder whether the real
question is "Why *won't* I hear God's voice?" The Scriptures present
a God who speaks to humanity regularly, in a myriad of different
ways, and yet who charges us with not listening. The psalmist
pleads, "O that today you would listen to his voice! Do not harden
your hearts" (Psalm 95:7-8). Spiritual deafness is not an issue with
the ability of the ear to hear but with the softness of the heart.
Those of us who live in this intimately personal universe are called
to open up our hearts and listen.

The personal demands that listening places on us lead us to erect
roadblocks for self-protection. Listening surfaces our feelings of
powerlessness, and so we marshal psychological and theological
reasoning to restore our sense of strength. One common expla-
nation for why we need not bother with the notion that God
speaks directly to our lives is that the Bible contains all the revelation we require. Perhaps ancient believers needed to hear God in

other ways, but now that his word has been canonized we no longer have such need. Some would say that to place an emphasis on any other of God's communication styles is to question the sufficiency of the Bible.

I am concerned that restricting God's self-communication to words written on papyrus thousands of years ago opens our faith to becoming as dusty as some of our study Bibles. Giving the Bible an esteemed place cannot mean muzzling God's personal word that he continues to speak to the church. We cannot hide behind our Bibles to shield us from the immediacy of God's voice. Dallas Willard is right that the Bible is the "permanent address for the Word of God," but, I would add, God is always on the move. Scripture itself testifies to numerous ways that God reveals himself. God's personal speech will not contradict the Bible, interpreted as a whole, and will often be spoken into our lives through the words of the biblical authors. However, to fully submit to the Scriptures will mean listening to the God they testify to, the One who lives in vibrant relationship with his people. Only then will we have upheld the sacred character of the Bible.

Listening to the Scriptures is how we familiarize ourselves with God's voice. We come face to face, and ear to mouth, with our Creator, Redeemer and Sustainer. The Bible should never close us to hearing God's voice in other venues; rather it ought to open us to recognize it wherever we hear it. In a sense, the Scriptures are a tuning fork for adjusting our ears to the tone of God's voice. It attunes us to the quality, the pitch and the cadence of God's voice, and to the character that his voice expresses, so that we can identify his true voice over false ones.

We must guard against limiting God's speech or restricting the arenas in which he can speak with us. Sometimes it seems like you can distinguish various Christian traditions by how it is they claim

God speaks to us. One church will say God speaks most pointedly in public worship, another most fully in the sacraments. One tradition will claim God speaks through one leader, another will say group consensus. One body will say God only speaks in the Scriptures, another will say God also speaks in the tradition handed on to us. One will say God speaks in silent contemplation, another will say in loud tongues. One church says God is a prolific talker, another says he is the strong and silent type.

I suspect that many of the theological arguments leveled against the idea that God speaks personally to us today are well-reasoned smokescreens for fear. I understand this fear. There is probably no more enthralling—and mysterious—topic than the nature of God's communication with humanity, and few are immune to its lure and even its abuse. Throughout the centuries people have done destructive and horrific things all because, they claimed, God told them to. Wars have been waged by two sides both claiming they were inspired by a word from the Lord. People have claimed that God revealed a new truth to them that contradicts the historical confessions of faith that bind the church together. Charismatic leaders have been anointed as God's spokesmen by fawning masses who were deluded by a dictator's power. Because of these crimes, both historical and contemporary, we have developed a simple and trusted formula: "God spoke to me" equals "I'm a crazy person."

Another way this fear expresses itself is when groups develop hierarchies of listening, in which certain people are entrusted with a privileged place to hear from God. A leader, assumed to have the best set of spiritual ears, is anointed to hear the word of God for others. It's a win-win: he (it's almost always a he) amasses power and wealth while the people in the community are protected from having to hear directly from God. People will pay extravagant amounts of money to avoid being pursued by the Hound of

Heaven.[4] Many people are genuinely afraid of the idea of God speaking, since it seriously threatens their sense of control, but I wonder if the greater fear is this: What if God won't speak *to me*? Who am I, in my insignificant and wayward life, that the Creator of the universe would see fit to communicate with me? At least if I delegate the task of listening to someone else, I won't have to endure the disapproving silences.

To be clear, there *should* be a healthy dose of fear in listening to God's voice. When the Creator speaks, the creation shivers. It's a dangerous business when people start listening to God for themselves instead of being told what he is saying to them. We also know our own tendencies toward self-deception and how easy it is to imagine a divine authorship for what are really our own hopes, fears and dreams.[5] But we cannot allow fear to plug our ears to the sound of God's voice. Further, we cannot allow fear to prevent us from the exhilaration, joy and adventure that fills a life marked by listening to God. To live the listening life is to open ourselves to surprise, to our routines being interrupted, and to paths we did not intend to walk but that arrive at places of breathtaking beauty we might have missed.

LISTENING FILTERS

In the Scriptures God communicates with humans so widely that I believe the burden of proof lies firmly on those who claim God has ceased to speak. Throughout the Old and New Testaments God employs an impressive arsenal of communication tools: words spoken from heaven, words written on tablets, preaching and prophetic words, answered prayer, visual demonstrations, counsels and consensus, thoughts, dreams, visions, symbols, words from others, signs in creation, angels, music and song, spiritual gifts, the breaking of bread and immersion in river water, common sense, conviction of sin, impressions on the conscience, and of course, a chatty donkey. The Bible does not offer a systematic treatment for how God speaks and how to recognize his voice. It assumes that God speaks in manifold and mysterious and unexpected ways. God speaks from outside and God speaks from within, God asks questions and gives answers, God speaks in noise and in silence. The universe crackles with the sound of God's voice.

I am prepared to take a liberal position on God's voice and his communications to his creation. God wants to be known and speaks freely, in a multitude of different ways. I believe all these means of hearing God's voice are fair game. This entire book is about listening to God because God's voice fills the universe, and when we listen to any agent we are potentially listening to God. Such a position may make me the most raging charismatic the Presbyterian Church has ever known. But if we want to confess God as truly sovereign, then his means of communication must be unrestricted, and they certainly cannot be less than what the Bible testifies to.

The answer to our nervousness, and a checkered past of misguided listeners, is not to attempt to muzzle God. When baseball's pioneers were beaned in the head, they didn't cancel the game or get a softer ball; they put on helmets and swung away. The answer is to have safeguards for interpreting God's voice. Let's not overcompensate by limiting God's ability and means for speaking to us; instead, let's limit our interpretations of his communications and what we do with them. We are unfiltered in our receiving of God's self-communications, but we are finely filtered in our responses to them.

The collective wisdom of our ancestors emphasizes three filters for testing the authenticity of what we have heard: harmony with Scripture, confirmation of community and pause of reflection.

First, what we hear has to sound like the God of the Bible. If it is inconsistent with the voice we meet in the Scriptures, then we know it is inauthentic. More specifically, we must listen through a Christ-filter, remembering that Jesus said Scripture spoke of and pointed to him. The written Word of God is summed up in the person of Jesus, the living and incarnate Word of God. In him we have heard the true Voice, and all communications we receive must harmonize with his voice. Any voice that calls for self-aggrandizement, personal glory and wealth, and power over others and that steers us away from the self-emptying of the cross comes from the father of lies, not our heavenly Father. Any voice that does not have the qualities of the fruit of the Spirit—love, joy, peace, patience, kindness, generosity, faithfulness—cannot be the voice of the Lord.

Second, we do not listen alone. We immerse ourselves in a listening community and filter what we hear through our fellow listeners. Listening is a communal exercise, and we are rightly suspicious when people hear God's direction to them in isolation. People that hear from God on an island have nowhere to go but into their own egos. God gives words to individuals not only for their own sake but for the benefit of their communities, strengthening faith and confirming callings. We need the soundboards of others to reflect back what they have heard, to confirm the words we have been given.

Third, we need to reflect on what we hear. Often God's voice carries such a weight to it that we are disposed to act immediately on it. A barking command from the officer in charge is likely to make the soldiers jump. God's word is usually meant to be the beginning of a new conversation, not the end. It may be unexpected and cut against the grain, but it usually is not intended to override common sense and careful reasoning. Plus, to my chagrin, God has a tendency to speak in ways that don't bring total clarity, offering one step rather than tracing a clear horizon for the future. His word requires consideration and careful reflection. We bring all our senses and faculties to bear in the reflection process: reason, feelings, intuition, the impact on others and the future decisions that will be required by such a response. Patience is our ally and our guard against rash action, because the careful treatment of God's personal word may require us to wait.

THE VOICE HEARD AT CARL'S JR

Kathi heard her call to Ireland while eavesdropping at Carl's Jr. At an adjacent booth a missionary to Ireland on furlough talked to a friend about her ministry. Kathi was spellbound. Over the next few days, she couldn't let it go. She still can't. She tracked down that missionary and met with her for two hours, and in that conversation, she reports, "God gave me a love for the people of Ireland, and that has not stopped." The call in her was growing, and she knew that she had to gather others to help her listen.

A Quaker, Kathi called together what her tradition calls a "clearness committee." A group of trusted friends gather around the person making the decision, but they are not there to give advice. They ask questions, they listen and they sit in silence. How refreshing. Her confidants asked Kathi questions about her process of arriving at this sense of call, her motivations, what Scriptures were informing her decision and how God was speaking to her. Mostly, they asked questions about timing. Her father had just died, her grandmother was sick and she was a semester away from finishing her master's of social work. Kathi desperately wanted to go Ireland immediately, but she felt compelled to wait for one year, which sounded interminable to her at the time. She later acknowledged that while she had a heart that was burning for Ireland, she had a lack of clarity. She told me,

"The Holy Spirit isn't confused, and so if we have a lack of clarity, we need to wait."

NEW CREATION EARS

I am convinced that a listening, conversational relationship with God is supposed to be the most natural thing in the world. In the first two chapters of Genesis, in both creation stories, the first thing that humans do is *hear* the commands of God. A chapter later, we are given the delightful anthropomorphism of God strolling in the late afternoon, searching out a conversation with the people he created. Tragically, he finds his creatures hiding from him, guilty of listening to the wrong voices: the tantalizing voice of the serpent and the deliciousness of their own pride. And thus an easy listening relationship with God became the exception rather than the rule. The original sin passed on to their ancestors centers on an inability to listen to the Creator.

Thankfully God does not leave us deaf. Eugene Peterson does some outstanding exegetical work with a verse in Psalm 40, which is often translated "my ears you have opened" (v. 6); but, Peterson explains, the Hebrew literally reads "my ears you have *dug.*" In a beautiful and painful image, God takes a spade to our skulls and digs out ear holes. The metaphor says two things: First, hearing is a gift, a work of God. In a world that has fallen from a natural listening relationship with God, we rely on the work of the Holy Spirit to reopen our ears. And second, we have hard heads. God didn't scoop out ears like ice cream; he *dug* them. Other translations say that God "pierced my ears," as if he took a pickaxe to our heads or perhaps a stick of dynamite that jolted our eardrums out of their stupor. The prophet Isaiah declared that God *awakens his ear*: "Morning by morning he wakens—*wakens* my ear to listen as those who are taught" (Isaiah 50:4, italics added). God issues a wake-up call to us each morning, dragging us out of bed by our ears, so that we may hear and live as we are called.

We who are united with Christ in his resurrection are new creations. The package of new creation comes with new ears enclosed, specially tuned to the pitch-perfect tone of God's voice. The old holes had closed and turned in on themselves, merely echoing the sound of our own egos and selfish interests. They were responsible for a type of vertigo that had thrown our lives off-kilter. Physiologically speaking, vertigo is a dysfunction of the inner ear that produces dizziness and a consequent lack of balance. Spiritually speaking, the old, damaged inner ears caused our lives to wobble and stumble, disoriented and tossed to and fro by a cacophony of voices. But God has dug new holes, clearing out the debris of sin and the dirt of the old self, letting in the sounds of new life. Our new ears are reopened to easy conversation with God and enable us to respond obediently to his calls and commands. We can now walk the straight line of righteousness.

Life with new creation ears promises even greater intimacy. The relationship with God depicted in the New Testament, secured by the work of Christ, is so intimate as to blur the lines between subject and object. A cornerstone of the apostle Paul's theology is that we are "in Christ," united to him in such a personal and profound way that our lives interpenetrate with Jesus' life. This personal interweaving draws us into the deepest relational nexus of all: the relationship between Father, Son and Holy Spirit. The lines between God and humanity cannot be so neatly drawn any longer because the life of God is lived *in us,* and the Voice of God is spoken *in us and through us.* A dialogue is not only happening between God and us; the very conversation of God, the trinitarian tria-logue, is carrying on inside of us.

A conversation between the persons of the Trinity is now passing through us.[6] In other words, listening is not first our practice or labor; listening is something that happens in us, even when we are not consciously aware of it. We can trust that we will hear the Father because the Spirit of his Son dwells in us and listens on our behalf. And we can trust that the Father will hear us because his Spirit is crying out in us: "And because you are children, God has sent the Spirit of his Son into our hearts, crying, 'Abba! Father!'" (Galatians 4:6). Consider one more text:

> Likewise the Spirit helps us in our weakness; for we do not know how to pray as we ought, but that very Spirit intercedes with sighs too deep for words. And God, who searches the heart, knows what is the mind of the Spirit, because the Spirit intercedes for the saints according to the will of God. (Romans 8:26-27)

These verses are often invoked when a person is in crisis and finds herself unable to articulate her prayer. The Spirit offers up intercessory groans that are intelligible to the Father. But there is something even more remarkable here. When we enter into prayer, no matter what the circumstances, we step into a conversation that has been happening since the foundation of the world but is now happening not only apart from us but *through* us. The Spirit groans in us, the Son intercedes in us, the Father listens to us. We have been drawn into the heart of the trinitarian conversation. Our existence has become an enfleshed, walking conversation.

CLOSE YOUR EARS AND LISTEN

We are called to partner with God in keeping our new creation ears open. When we give other voices that war against God sway in our lives, or if we make a good voice that is not God preeminent, our ears close a little. For example, Jesus drove a wedge between God and wealth: "No one can serve two masters; for a slave will either hate the one and love the other, or be devoted to the one and despise the other. You cannot serve God and wealth" (Matthew 6:24). You cannot listen simultaneously to the voices of two masters. Jesus' kingdom announcement, and his cry to "repent and believe," was a summons to turn from the alternative voices you are following to hear the one true voice of the King. We could paraphrase "repent and believe" as "close your ears and listen." Obedience has both a stop and a start to it. We turn our backs to the old voices and offer our attention to Jesus' voice.

We desire for God's voice to crescendo in our lives, with the competing voices fading away. This means that we must ruthlessly silence the calls of other masters. We confess our auditory rebellions to others, since somehow moving the jaw in confession seems to unplug our ears. Most importantly, we must let God define himself. We have to fight the temptation to simply add a couple of God's songs to our playlists—Jehovah's greatest hits. We must put away our convenient notions of God—the one who always agrees with us, the one who always favors our nation or political agenda, the one who feeds us candy and never vegetables. Louis Evely put it this way: "[God's] language isn't ours. It isn't what we expect. Only when we love him enough to prefer his ways to ours, his language to ours, and his will to ours, only then will we discover him."[7] To hear him and to know him we must allow him to speak on his own terms.

THE GOD SONG

What do you think God sounds like? The very first time we encounter God's voice is as Creator. Genesis opens on a scene of deep, ancient silence. When God's voice breaks in with "Let there be light," how do you hear it? Is it a rumbling vocal thunderclap, a sonic boom of speech that scatters the seas and jolts the land into place? Do you hear it as the voice of an artist who thoughtfully and quietly paints words on a silent canvas? Perhaps you hear a whisper, the nudge of a Creator who feels no need to shout.

I wonder, along with much smarter people such as C. S. Lewis, if the Creator *sang* the creation into existence.[8] The genre of the creation story is poetry, and song is poetry put to music. All the lyrical components are present—the metaphors, the short phrasing, the alliteration, the refrains of "And God said" and "And God saw that it was good." The discordant and unrecognizable notes of the watery chaos are pulled together to play a creation symphony, God singing the elements to rest.

We find God singing in another place in the Scriptures. In the prophetic book Zephaniah, God first mourns the rebelliousness of Jerusalem: "Ah, soiled, defiled, oppressing city! It has listened to no voice; it has accepted no correction. It has not trusted in the LORD; it has not drawn near to its God" (Zephaniah 3:1-2). God vows to judge the pridefulness of the city that will not listen, and his voice will come with a fiery passion that will burn away its callous façade. But after the judgment comes . . . singing. "The LORD, your God, is in your midst, a warrior who gives victory; he will rejoice over you with gladness, he will renew you in his love; *he will exult over you with loud singing*" (Zephaniah 3:17, italics added).

It is an excruciatingly beautiful image. The battle is won, Jerusalem is reclaimed, and the Lord sings lustily in his city. This is no sappy love ballad or fluffy campfire song. This is the Victor snatching up his people and singing loudly over them, a chorus of fierce love and redemption.

Does your God sing? When God sings, chaos retreats and his people are swept up in his love. Can you hear him singing over you, his beloved? When you do, the other songs fade away. Yet too often we hear his voice as a cosmic dictator, a disapproving parent or the prickly voice on our shoulder that says "No!" No wonder we don't trust him. Our desire to listen is shaped by the trust we have for the voice we hear. What if we could hear God singing over us and all creation, calling us his own? Henri Nouwen counseled us to "listen to the voice who calls you the beloved, because otherwise you will run around begging for affirmation, for praise, and for success."[9] When we have heard his call of "beloved," we will be much more willing to heed his calls to decision and action.

Our context for listening to God's call is an ongoing, vibrant, growing relationship with our heavenly Father. We do not seek disembodied instructions, timeless and faceless principles, or prepackaged life answers that we can pull out when required. Those are too easily controlled and can be manipulated to justify all kinds of behaviors. Abstract moralizing falls away before the voice of a living Lord who addresses us personally and who calls us to faithfulness in our time and place. We are wooed, not merely informed. As Dallas Willard puts it, "Our communion with God must be the context for our communications with God."[10] That way, when we confront a season of pain or a significant decision, we do not try to summon guidance out of the air. We are drawing from a past of walking with the Lord, of familiarity with Jesus and of meditating on the Scriptures. We work with memories of his prior words to us and the ways he has shown us mercy, which help us both interpret our present circumstances and hear a fresh word spoken to us. In an ongoing listening relationship with the Lord we may find that our confusion in new situations decreases, our fear abates more quickly and our perseverance is more than we expected. What previously felt like an "emergency" might seem less urgent and threatening.

LISTENING WITH YOUR FEET

"In the beginning was the Word, and the Word was with God, and the Word was God. . . . And the Word became flesh and lived among us, and we have seen his glory, the glory as of a father's only son, full of grace and truth" (John 1:1, 14). The Gospel writer John gives us a picture of a word that is not mere breath passing through teeth and gums. He presents us with a word that *acts*, that accomplishes something. God's works are speech-acts. It invokes God's declaration in the prophet Isaiah:

> For my thoughts are not your thoughts,
>   nor are your ways my ways, says the LORD.
> For as the heavens are higher than the earth,
>   so are my ways higher than your ways
>   and my thoughts than your thoughts.
>
> For as the rain and the snow come down from heaven,
>   and do not return there until they have watered the earth,
> making it bring forth and sprout,
>   giving seed to the sower and bread to the eater,
> so shall my word be that goes out from my mouth;
>   it shall not return to me empty,
> but it shall accomplish that which I purpose,
>   and succeed in the thing for which I sent it. (Isaiah 55:8-11)

The nature of God's transcendence, and what separates his words from human words, is not just that God is smarter than we are; it's that God's speech has efficacy. His word has a substance and a power to it, and it has the capacity to actually effect what he desires. God does not just do what he says; *what he says, does.*

God's word is an agent, even a personality, present since the very beginning and in the fullness of time revealed to be the Son. Now we know that the Word of God is first and foremost a person. In the person of Jesus, the wisdom that holds the universe together is incarnate, the invisible married to the visible, and God's speech takes on flesh. God's message to the world walked around and taught and ate and slept and now intercedes in the divine throne room.

The implication for listening is this: If God's self-communication comes in the form of a person, then the nature of our listening must be equally embodied. Our listening must be as incarnate as the Word that has been spoken to us. In a way, our whole lives become ears, receivers for the Word of God. When Jesus says, "Follow me," we do not only listen with our ears and minds. We listen as a sprinter in the blocks listens for the starter's pistol, muscles taut, poised for action. You've heard the phrase "you vote with your feet"? Well, you also listen with your feet.

TONE OF VOICE

One of the marks of his followers, says Jesus, will be that they recognize his voice when he calls. The shepherd knows the name of each of his sheep, and they know his voice (John 10:4). They will run from the voices of strangers and to the voice that they know, like a child runs to her daddy when she hears him arrive home.

Years ago, I was exhilarated to read in Dallas Willard's book *Hearing God* that God's voice is recognizable and has predictable components to it, like any other voice. It has a tone, weight, volume and content. Of course! I had been learning for years that God has a personality, a reliable and unchanging character, but it had never occurred to me that that personality came with a particular voice. God's voice does not waver, stutter or change. It is as consistent as his character. Willard quotes Stanley Jones, who distinguishes between the voice of the subconscious and the voice of God speaking within: "Perhaps the rough distinction is this: The voice of the subconscious argues with you, tries to convince you; but the inner voice of God does not argue, does not try to convince you. It just speaks, and it is self-authenticating. It has the feel of the voice of God within it."[11]

A few years ago I was driving home after spending Christmas with my family. I was alone with my post-holiday thoughts, which were racing much faster than the seventy miles per hour my Honda CR-V was doing. I had been effectively unemployed for the past year and a half. "Effectively unemployed" is another way of saying "trying to write for a living." I had been laid off from my hospice chaplaincy job two summers before, which sparked the revelation that I could "live the dream" as a writer! It wasn't going well. This wasn't the swanky, jet-setting lifestyle I'd anticipated. There were sidewalk lemonade stands that were more profitable than I was.

I had kept the anxiety at bay pretty well, but that night, for some reason, I was in its throes. Henri Nouwen's picture of the inner world of "monkeys jumping up and down in banana trees"[12] was terrifyingly true during that drive. My monkeys were not just jumping up and down and eating bananas; they were throwing feces and presenting their backsides. Questions battled with potential solutions but only despair seemed to be winning, and I was begin . . .

DO NOT WORRY ABOUT MONEY.

My inner world fell silent. The other voices fled from the Voice like the waves of the Red Sea. It didn't shout or scold or repeat itself, but it carried an unmistakable weight and confidence. Plus, the words sounded awfully familiar. In the Sermon on the Mount, Jesus counseled his disciples: "Do not worry about your life, what you will eat or what you will drink, or about your body, what you will wear" (Matthew 6:25). I had not been thinking about that text recently, but I knew it authenticated the Voice that I heard. It was not a word that I expected, but it was as if my soul had been waiting for it in order to come home.

Even as I write this, I can still feel the impression that short, simple statement made on me. It did not answer my questions or change my circumstances—I was not offered a job for another year—and yet somehow the anxiety melted away and was replaced by a lingering peace. Peace is one of those fruits of the Spirit that God's voice instills. His voice has an authority that creates realities in the person who listens and belief in what is said.

I am convinced that we know God's voice as much by its impact on us as by the profundity of the words themselves. God's words seem to reach a place in our hearts and minds that no other voice can reach, even a place that transcends language. I have had many experiences of God's presence—some with words and some wordless—in which the *force* of presence is more impactful and memorable than any words that accompany it. The words may dissipate, but the effect lingers in the body's memory. The body trembles, but it is not a fearful tremble. It is more like the chills a groom experiences when he sees his bride walking down the aisle. The occasion is so weighty, so beautiful, so hopeful, that the body responds physically and emotionally. Perhaps those moments don't occur often, but when they do, they change us.

We may later report what we heard to someone, only to find our words fall flat. I suppose that if even the Spirit resorts to groans, the odds of us finding the appropriate words are slim. This is one of the reasons why we may choose to guard our stories of hearing from God carefully. Richard Foster, in his book on meditative prayer, *Sanctuary of the Soul*, encourages us to be circumspect about our experiences of God's presence. Our inability to capture the experience in words has a way of instilling doubt that anything even happened or that it was as significant as it seemed at the time. But the impact on the body and soul remains.

HEARING GOD'S VOICE

If God is in the business of communicating with his people, and his voice has certain distinguishable properties, why do we still struggle to hear it? In some cases it is simply a lack of training. Dallas Willard believes that many people regularly hear from God but don't actually know it. God's voice enters as a thought or an impression on their consciousness, and they respond to it yet do not ascribe the inner voice to its proper source. As incredible as that sounds, as I reflect on the voices I have listened to in times of critical decision, I think I agree with Willard. There have been many occasions in which I wrestled and listed the pros and cons and sought counsel, yet attained no clarity whatsoever until a moment in which I suddenly *knew* what to do. The inspiration would often flash when I was in a detached state of mind, not even thinking about the issue at hand. It was as though the thought did not originate with my mind, as if the decision just happened to me.

There are other causes of our inability to hear and identify God's voice. One paradox that emerges in this discussion is this: we may not hear from God because our lives are too loud. Or, we may not hear from God because our lives are too quiet.

Too loud. You can only hear it in the quietest hour of the night. During the day, as you move and talk and eat, it is constant but imperceptible. But when you put the side of your head on your pillow and let your breathing slow as you fall into unconsciousness, you may hear it: the tiny, rhythmic pulsation of your heart beating blood into your body, a pounding whisper that keeps you alive even when you're asleep.

When God's voice creeps up on us like a heartbeat in the dark, it is often referred to in our tradition as "the still, small voice." God speaks in myriad ways, and even occasionally shouts, but the testimony of countless believers throughout the ages has emphasized the still, small voice as one of the most important ways God speaks to us. The Quakers call this voice "the inner teacher." Others have called it the inner word or the inner voice, received by the inner ear. John Calvin called it "the inner testimony of the Holy Spirit."[13] Dallas Willard described it as a direct impression on a person's consciousness, usually expressed as a thought, with a certain force and weight, occurring in a person's mind.[14]

The phrase "still, small voice" comes from the King James Version's rendering of the "sheer silence" in the Elijah story, an interpretation that isn't the best translation of the Hebrew but that does represent well the nature of God's communications with us. The sovereign King of the universe, to our surprise, does not often trumpet his message to his subjects. God's volume knob is rarely turned all the way to the right; his voice in our ears is subtle, restrained, even easy to miss.

Why would God speak so softly in a world that so often needs a blaring wake-up call? I have to conclude that God's speech patterns indicate how important he considers our listening. If God shouted, listening would not be required, but a whisper forces us to pay attention and to strain to hear his voice. A whispered message assumes that the listener is in proximity to the speaker. The closeness required by a whisper requires that we are in close relationship with the Lord, aware of his presence and walking with him, poised to do what he says. God's hushed tones also necessitate that we are quiet and still enough to recognize him. T. S. Eliot said

it well: "Where shall the word be found, where will the word resound? Not here, there is not enough silence."[15]

One of the questions I have wrestled with is, why does it seem
like the figures in biblical stories hear from God so much more
than we do? Is it a matter of worldview? Did the ancients attribute
everything in the natural world to the influence of the heavens
because of a pre-scientific worldview? The heavens seemed to
speak so fluently then. Thunder expressed the anger of the gods. A
good harvest revealed God's pleasure. I expect that differing worldviews do play a part. I wonder, though, if God's relative silence in
our day can be traced to another source. Perhaps our ancestors
didn't have the same luxury of distraction. Their inability to escape
into television or the Internet, their relatively few choices for entertainment, the lack of electrifying stimuli, their agrarian labors
that stopped at sundown, their slow pace of life and the quiet of a
pre-industrial night might have helped draw their attention to the
heavens. The stars are much brighter when you're not looking at
them through lights and smog.

A loud, overcrowded, hyperactive life is the antithesis of the
listening life. The hyperactive life is so often trying to prove its
worth, make its mark and justify its existence. The listening life
waits, quietly and humbly, for God to make his mark on us.

John Coltrane, legendary jazz saxophonist, made his mark on
the jazz world by improvising at breakneck speed. No one had ever
seen a musician who could play and move his fingers so feverishly.
Soon he was playing gigs with the superstars of his day and
changing the way people understood the genre. Unfortunately,
much of the frenzy that marked Coltrane's style was the result of
the substances in his system.[16] In 1957, his system ravaged by drugs
and alcohol, and his career and life on the brink of collapse, Coltrane went to his mother's house and sought God in the quiet of

his room. According to pastor and jazz aficionado Robert Gelinas, "Four days later, he emerged a changed man, for—according to him—God had met him in a most unusual way. It was a sound, a droning resonance, a reverberation, unlike anything he had ever heard."[17] God's presence had come to John Coltrane as a sound.

Not only did this divine groove change his life, it changed the way he played. The frantic improvisation was replaced by a slow, soulful style, in which Coltrane listened for the God sound to come again and tried to replicate it on his sax. Gelinas explains that "he came to believe that if he could play that sound for others, then they, too, could experience what he had experienced during those four days in his bedroom."[18] For the rest of his life Coltrane sought to find that music that had healed him, and while he was never able to rediscover it, he recorded one of the best-selling jazz albums of all time, *A Love Supreme*, during this musical pilgrimage. The four parts of *A Love Supreme* follow a pilgrim on his journey toward God:

1. "Acknowledgement"—The recognition of God

2. "Resolution"—Commitment to seek God

3. "Pursuance"—The journey toward God

4. "Psalm"—Celebration of the discovery of God[19]

John Coltrane discovered that listening to God required a slow movement and a quiet search. In our pursuit of God, we may discover that a hectic pace of life, while having all the marks of success and productivity, is too loud with the sound of our own voice. Like Coltrane, we may have to retreat into the quiet of our rooms and into slower rhythms in order to truly listen.

Too quiet. The claim that God's voice cannot be heard among the clamor of modern life is a common one. But I have also come to realize that there is a life that is *too quiet* to hear God's voice. This is because God's communications are not haphazard. The Holy Spirit, it turns out, is not a hapless talk show host nattering about everything under the sun, hoping that a few people will tune in to the right frequency. Instead, God's word comes most often to a certain kind of person seeking to lead a certain kind of life. Dallas Willard put it this way: "Our union with God . . . consists chiefly in a conversational relationship with God while we are *each consistently and deeply engaged as his friend and colaborer in the affairs of the kingdom of the heavens.*"[20]

As much as I enjoy the idea of sitting with God on a porch swing, sipping lemonade and chatting about the weather, the better image may be a soldier in the heat of battle, in constant communication with his commanding officer. The soldier doesn't just want to hear from his superior, he *needs* to. He is in over his head, seeking to complete the mission he has been given, in urgent need of guidance and support. As Eric Metaxas put it, "When God speaks to you, you know you're going to need it."[21]

God does not speak in an arbitrary language to whomever happens to be listening at the time. God's language is faith, hope and love. If we are seeking to lead a life marked by believing, hoping and loving, moving with the Lord in his mission and work, then we can have the expectation that the Lord will speak to us and give us what we need. On the other hand, if we sit still and refuse to act until we are explicitly told to act, we may be waiting for a very long time. Sometimes our cell phones have no signal in the shelter of our homes, and we need to get out and move in order to get reception.

I'm also convinced that listening to God is not unlike writing: if I were to wait to write until inspiration struck, I would write practically nothing. But if I chain myself to my desk every morning at 8:00 A.M. and start typing something—anything—inspiration has a way of unexpectedly pulling up a chair. If we act on what we know, maintaining a posture of listening, the One who is with us until the end of the age will come. And when he does speak with us, we must be prepared to act on it. Karl Barth said that the best way to test the authenticity of a communication from God is to act on it and see what happens.[22]

PRAYER AS LISTENING

Those of us who come from an evangelical tradition have grown accustomed to a certain glibness in speaking about God. We love to share and testify and pray aloud, and our prayers are often peppered with the repetition of God's name—in case others forget, in our long-winded ways, who we are praying to. But I have found, over the years, that I have grown more restrained both in my speech *about* God and in my speech *to* God. I share fewer of my experiences with others, and I have come to see prayer more as a way of being with God and less as an opportunity to talk. Jews, both ancient and contemporary, have avoided saying God's proper name, and I find myself drawn to Christian traditions that approach God in a more circumspect way. I am more attracted to ancient ways of prayer, which always seem to be quieter and less urgent than those I experience in many evangelical contexts.

Endless words spoken in a heavenly direction—prayer soliloquies—have a way of closing us to the relationship that is offered to us. We all know people, even well-intentioned ones, who habitually dominate conversations, and we can walk away from those conversations feeling more distant from that person than we did before the conversation. For a tradition known for its emphasis on personal relationship with Jesus, evangelicals are not exactly known for their listening abilities. Yet listening is how you get to know a person. You can't present a monologue to a person and have any confidence that you are learning anything about that person. It's in listening that you gain access to their mind, discover who they are and what they are like, and whether they can be trusted.

The relatively new category of "listening prayer" has been developed in response to the listening gap in evangelical practice. In contrast to talking methods of prayer, listening prayer seeks to discern God's voice through Scripture and direct listening. While I have benefited greatly from these practices, I find it revealing that we even have a designation in Christian circles for "listening prayer." It indicates that listening belongs to a special kind of prayer, perhaps reserved for people who have achieved an elite status in the spiritual life. The assumption seems to be that normal prayer is talking prayer. Day after day we leave words on the altar, hoping that God will sweep them up and consider them. Listening is an afterthought.

I would contend that prayer without listening is not truly prayer. I see no other way that we can be faithful to Paul's injunction to "pray without ceasing" unless we understand prayer as listening and all of life as the context for listening prayer. Yes, we offer intercession, praise and petition, but they originate out of our listening. To treat prayer as listening is to acknowledge that God always has the first word, that we are products of his creative word and that the universe is held together by his sustaining word. He has spoken the Alpha, knows the day when he will shout the Omega, and our present lives are engaged in listening for the rest of his letters.

In prayer we offer our ears and whole selves to God, in all of life's contingencies, whether we're in a quiet chapel or a noisy crowd. We do not have to fight for particular situations or seek out the perfect atmosphere for listening. Listening is not reserved for the spiritual aristocracy. Listening is about more than straining to hear voices; it's about preparing the conditions of our hearts, cultivating an openness inside us. In this way, listening is a *posture*, one of availability and surrender. We don't control how or when God will speak, but we can control the acoustics that receive the sound. We want to prepare an inner place that is open and hospitable to God's voice. That inner place requires humility, patience, attentiveness and trust. We must have hearts already surrendered in order to recognize his voice when he calls.

Specific times devoted to listening prayer, once we embrace whole-life listening, are exercises for hearing God's voice in all spheres of life. In quieting ourselves before the Lord we detach from the power of other voices and attach to our Lord's voice. Over time the other voices become quieter and less urgent. Nouwen said, "The task is to persevere in my solitude, to stay in my cell until all my seductive visitors get tired of pounding on my door and leave me alone."[23] In those rare moments when we are able to sit in the quiet, release the noise and the anxieties that drive us into noise, and attune ourselves to God, we are training, preparing ourselves to be listeners in all of life.

It must be acknowledged, however, that the vast majority of the time, when we settle ourselves in to listen to the Lord in a time of devoted prayer, we will hear *nothing*. This is discouraging for newcomers, especially when others seem to be having exhilarating experiences with the Lord. We must remember that we are not ultimately seeking the spectacular, nor anxiously straining for a word from the Lord, but we are seeking the Lord himself. The listening life is based less on the content heard and more on relationship with the One who speaks. Like Elijah, we can even come to listen for the silences, because God's silences have a different texture to them. His silences are full. When they come, we know the story is not over.

EVERYDAY LISTENING

Listening to God is an everyday reality. In the seventeenth century a monk named Brother Lawrence sought to practice the presence of God in the most ordinary situations. Lawrence was as compelling as he was unimpressive. For years his main monastic duty was to wash dishes in the monastery's kitchen. But what he understood that so many over the centuries have missed is that God is no less present in the pedestrian chore than he is in the dazzling performance. This is why most of the best Christians are people we'll never hear about. Lawrence grasped that when God is with us, an old, dark kitchen is a ground as holy as a stained-glass-encased chapel. The mystic Teresa of Ávila said that "God walks among the pots and pans."[24] We are invited to listen not as a teleport into some ethereal world but as a means of discovering God in the mundane.

Whitworth religion professor Jerry Sittser once calculated that the average person in his or her lifetime will spend 2,000 hours brushing his or her teeth, 14,600 hours driving, 43,800 hours eating, and 58,400 hours doing chores.[25] The most magical life will still mostly consist of absolutely ordinary activities. Our challenge is to learn how to listen when brushing our teeth, vacuuming and commuting.

There is an ancient prayer called the Jesus Prayer—"Lord Jesus Christ, Son of God, have mercy on me, a sinner"—that has been practiced in the Eastern Orthodox tradition since the Egyptian ascetics of the fifth century. The idea behind the prayer is that if a person repeats it continually throughout the day, she will become aware that reality is Jesus-soaked, that God is alive in every moment. Some devotees of the Jesus Prayer have repeated it thousands of times per day.

I have developed my own version of this prayer, which has

become the centerpiece of my prayer life. In the book of 1 Samuel the old priest Eli instructed the precocious prophet Samuel: "If [the Lord] calls you, you shall say, 'Speak, LORD, for your servant is listening'" (1 Samuel 3:9). And that has become my daily prayer. I call it the Samuel prayer, which is less clever than it is easy to remember. "Speak Lord, your servant is listening": these are the first words that I say when I wake up in the morning, the last words I say when I get into bed and my repeated offering throughout the day. To be honest, it flows more easily when I am writing, preaching or sitting in church. But I think it is more important to say when I am paying bills, cooking and scooping cat litter, as I need the reminder that the winds of the Spirit blow through every place and activity.

When I first started repeating this prayer, I feared I was in for disappointment. Is it presumptuous to assume God will speak to me throughout the day? The answer came quickly: yes, yes it is. I came to realize, however, that the Samuel prayer is not about convincing God to personally speak to me more often; it is a way of making space. It says, "Here I am" to God. I am opening my heart to God, preparing for when he says, "Here I am" in return.

Saying the Samuel prayer almost always causes me to take a deep breath, to slow down and become more attentive to what is taking place around me and in me. I become more aware of God's presence. This is a God-saturated moment. I start asking, "What is this moment teaching me?" rather than demanding things and manipulating situations to get what I want. My prayers become less about what I want and more about living in the presence of God.

Several times a week I also practice short blocks of silent prayer, usually five to ten minutes, which some traditions call centering prayer, allowing conscious thoughts to pass through my mind while holding to my anchor: "Speak, Lord, your servant is listening." The main purpose of these times is to enjoy the Lord and his presence in the same we would sit with a loved one in quiet intimacy. It's best to take this slowly, as a ten-minute block of sheer silence feels interminable at first. Start at two minutes and work your way up from there. One young mother I know practices centering prayer in the middle of the night while she rocks her baby back to sleep. In these times, God may speak directly to you, but most of the time he will not. Sometimes I think the Lord just wants me to learn stillness. I have learned not to despair when he does not speak, because I know that this is not the end of my listening life, but rather the beginning.

FOUR

Listening to Scripture

AFTER I GRADUATED FROM SEMINARY I stopped reading the Bible. It's been said that for all the gain that comes from dissecting a frog, all the hands-on knowledge one amasses from cutting out the organs and separating and scrutinizing the various parts, something still had to die in the process. My frog was dead. There is no doubt about that.

There had been a season before seminary when the Scriptures sang to me, angelic harmonies wafting through my life. The Word of God woke me up in the morning. In college, I used to rise at 6:30 in the morning—making me the first person awake on campus by about four hours—stroll into my drowsy, tree-lined town under an awakening California sun, and read my Bible through latté steam. One December morning I read Mary's Magnificat, and I'm sure that my heart leapt with Elizabeth's baby when he heard the voice of the woman who carried destiny inside her. I walked back to campus exulting with the mother of Jesus: my soul magnified the Lord, and my spirit rejoiced in God my Savior, you know that's right. Experiences like that made it seem like I floated to seminary on biblical sound waves, called to a life of studying and proclaiming the Scriptures. I couldn't imagine a more melodious life.

By the time I finished seminary, what had once sung three-part harmonies to me now sounded in the dry, unfeeling tones of a lecture hall. The Bible had become a specimen, and I had teased apart its components—all its grammatical, historical, textual, and cultural tendons and joints and blood vessels—until all connection and life was gone. The Magnificat lost its singing voice, fading before new life verses like

> The time is surely coming, says the Lord God,
>   when I will send a famine on the land;
> not a famine of bread, or a thirst for water,
>   but of hearing the words of the Lord.
> They shall wander from sea to sea,
>   and from north to east;
> they shall run to and fro, seeking the word of the Lord,
>   but they shall not find it. (Amos 8:11-12)

The word of God was elusive in those days. I still opened the Bible, even translated Greek and Hebrew, but it was a manual for preaching, a teacher's-edition textbook. I didn't read it as much as I used it. It was the word addressed to others, not to me, and my role was mediator, rarely receiver. Ambitious as I was back then, I tried to use the Bible as a ladder for climbing to the heights of preaching stardom, as a prop for displaying my own glamorous powers.[1] My treatment of the Bible was not unlike what the money changers did to the temple when they started peddling in its outer courts. They pre-empted a place of personal worship for a place of impersonal transaction. I'm afraid that for me the Bible had ceased to be a place of encounter and had become a place of business.

The problem with creating distance from the biblical text to see it more objectively is that you can end up distancing yourself from the One who spoke the word in the first place. When you put the

Bible on a slide and examine it under a microscope, you're the subject and the Bible is the object, an impersonal artifact to be studied. You can end up like Thomas Jefferson taking a razor to the Bible and excising all the miracle out of it.

I do not mean to attack biblical scholarship. All of us who read the Bible in our own language are absolutely dependent on the biblical scholars who gathered and translated that text. The problem that those of us who have spent time in scholarly circles face is not unlike the problem that engaged couples confront. Anyone who has planned a wedding will tell you that, from the moment the ring is placed on the woman's finger, it is remarkably easy to get lost in all the details of event planning. In all the negotiations about venue, flowers, invitations, food, guest lists, music, how to run interference with intrusive family members and the countless other details, many couples forget that a wedding is ultimately a personal and intimate encounter, an act of commitment between two people and the family and friends who confirm their vows. Our study of the Bible can be subject to the same depersonalizing forces. The Bible is a deeply personal book, a stage of encounter between God and his people, but the details of interpretation and the convoluted levels of methodology can crowd out its personality. We can get a fantastic wedding, but a poor marriage.

A PERSONAL WORD

The good news is this: in spite of all our attempts to create separation from the biblical text, the text itself speaks of a word that refuses our estrangement and even eliminates it. The mystery of the Word that originates from the Creator is that it reads us. You open the book, lay it down in front of you, but you instead discover that you have been opened, your soul laid bare by it. My subject to the Bible's object gets inverted and I become the Bible's object, arrested by it, revealed in it. I go to it as an actor reading a script but discover that I am the script and the Word acts on me. The law may have been written on tablets, but the word is now stitched into our hearts, shaping us and redefining us.

We often reserve the phrase "the Word of God" for the Bible, but the Bible itself actually testifies to God's "word" with rich and multifaceted imagery, extending far beyond the capacity we would normally ascribe to a word. For us, a word is a few squiggles on paper or a sound that rushes past us and disappears into space. In the Scriptures the word pulsates with life, action and enduring power.

The word sets our lives and our bodies on fire: Jeremiah said that "his word burns in my heart like a fire. It's like a fire in my bones" (Jeremiah 20:9 NLT). The word makes its home in us: Paul prayed for the Colossians that the word of Christ would *dwell* in them. God's word is succulent and nourishing: Isaiah instructs his listeners to *listen* diligently and *eat* what is good. The word is a seed planted in our hearts, growing new life: Peter says, "You have been born anew, not of perishable but of imperishable seed, through the living and enduring word of God." (1 Peter 1:23). The word dissects and examines us: Hebrews calls the word of God "sharper than any two-edged sword, piercing until it divides soul from spirit, joints from marrow; it is able to judge the thoughts and intentions of the heart" (Hebrews 4:12). The word grows in us and rescues us: James tells us to "welcome with meekness the implanted word that has the power to save your souls" (James 1:21).

If there is one common theme in these varied images, it is this: the word is something that gets inside of us, works its way organically through us and becomes part of us while it changes us. The word is personal, because it is a self-communication of the personal God and because it becomes a part of our personhood, moving and living with us. For those of us in Christ, when we read the Bible, the word planted in us recognizes the written word in the Scriptures. The word inside greets the word outside. We meet the God who spoke the word, and we meet our truest, deepest selves who are being rousted out of their slumber by the word inside.

THE LIFE MANAGEMENT BIBLE

When we open the Bible we risk true encounter, true relationship with the Lord of the universe and with our deep selves, and that can feel too dangerous. It can be too vulnerable, too uncertain, too frightening. But because we are good Christians committed to reading the Bible, we come up with ways to make it safer.

"Get familiar with this book," said the guest preacher holding up his tattered red leather Bible, "because it is a handbook for life management!" The woman sitting next to me in the pew audibly groaned, loud enough so that a few people turned their heads to look in our direction. I had to put my hand over my mouth to stifle my laughter. If I had known who the woman was, I doubt I would have been able to contain myself, because I learned after the service that she is a dignified, well-respected professor of preaching at a prestigious seminary. Together we sat through the rest of the sermon without further incident. The preacher was perfectly consistent in his life management biblical theology; he applied his chosen text to all sorts of practical matters, like diet, finances and national security.

Bumper-sticker theologians instruct us to read the Bible as "God's instruction manual" or to rely on it as a "safety net" that catches us when we would fall into sin and despair. Others teach us to open it like a medicine chest that holds cures for all spiritual ailments, or to treat it like an encyclopedia of collected religious knowledge. Michael Casey warns us against using the Bible like a recipe book for cooking up some contemplation, by which he seems to mean some felt presence of God.[2] More sophisticated approaches sometimes treat the Bible as a museum. The Scriptures house ancient relics, expressions of past cultures, historical records of primitive peoples, scratchings of dead dialects, which, as fascinating as they may be, belong in the past. But if we're honest, what all these methods have in common is that they protect us from personal encounter.

COMMUNICATING VERSUS WOOING

In the movie *Dead Poets Society*, John Keating, played by Robin Williams, asks his students, "Why was language invented?" His star student, Neil, ventures a guess: "To communicate?" to which Mr. Keating rejoins, "No! To woo women!" They're actually both right, but their interaction draws a line between two primary uses of language. The first use focuses on describing, and it sets out its content plainly and literally. This is the language of newspapers, instruction manuals and contracts. It is primarily concerned with questions of how and what, and it often progresses in steps: here's *how* you take this *what* and attach it to that *what* in order to get a nicely finished *what*. It is meant to transmit information in the most comprehensible and accessible fashion.

The second use of language not only describes but aims to convey the heart's knowledge. This is language that can be put to song. It is language dressed up, stirring with passion and longing, flirting with allusion, hints and subtext. It is a language of meeting: deeply personal, embedded in relationship or possible relationship. It makes for good poetry, and since no woman wants to receive a poem that describes her as literally as possible ("Your cheeks are red as a rose / you have many blackheads on your nose"), the poet intends not that she would learn as much as that she would swoon. Poetry and metaphor and song try to describe the indescribable, revealing what others may not be able to see.

If the first language discusses the world we already know, the second language opens up and invites us into worlds that we do not yet know.[3] As Mr. Keating explains, communication is absolutely necessary to sustain life, but passion and romance is what we stay alive for. This is the kind of language that has the power to transform us, not just enlighten us. It is captivated with questions of who, because those are questions of identity and relationship. Eugene Peterson explains that this sort of language seeks to form rather than inform: "When language is personal, which it is at its best, it reveals; and revelation is always formative—we don't know more, we become more. Our best users of language, poets and lovers and children and saints, use words to *make*—make intimacies, make character, make beauty, make goodness, make truth. . . . This is revelation, personally revealed."[4]

The Bible has much to teach us, it is true, about the nature of the universe, but so much of the Scriptures seem intent on wooing us rather than simply communicating to us. Our modern language fills how-to guides and instruction manuals for making life easier, but the Scriptures are saturated with stories, poetry, parables, songs and imagery that want to reveal a person, how he feels about us and how he is forming us in his image. Biblical revelation is less about *what* is revealed and more about *who* is revealed. Biblical revelation means that the temple curtain is torn, the glory is unleashed, and God is on the loose.

A PLACE OF ENCOUNTER

My reading of the Bible had been obstructed by impersonal approaches that treated the Bible as something to be used. What I had lost was the understanding that the Bible is a place of encounter. When we open the Scriptures, we are invited into a conversation, not only with the human authors but with the Author who dwells in and stands over the Scriptures. Jesus promised that the Holy Spirit would teach us everything and remind us of all he said, and I believe the Holy Spirit aids us in understanding and living the Bible (John 14:26). We never read the Bible alone.

The word we often use to capture the nature of the Bible, *inspired*, literally means "in-breathed," which takes us to Paul's description in 2 Timothy 3:16: "All scripture is inspired by God and is useful for teaching, for reproof, for correction, and for training in righteousness." Paul coins a new Greek word, *theopneustos*, translated into English as "inspired" but which literally means "God-breathed."[5] The words of the Scriptures are exhaled out of God's mouth. The Holy Spirit has often been called "the breath of God."

When we speak a word it rushes out of our mouths and vanishes, but when God speaks a word his very presence is carried along with it. God is never separate from his word. God's word is saturated and penetrated by God himself—his being, power and wisdom—so much so that you get a word that is a presence. It starts to make sense why the Gospel of John refers to Jesus, the eternal Son, as the Word of God. When you have words filled with the very being of God, you have a Word that *is* God.

Jesus Christ mediates not only our salvation but also our reading of the Bible. Beginning with the earliest Christian interpreters of the Bible, there has been a belief that Jesus is the protagonist not only of the New Testament but also of the Old Testament. All the Scriptures point to him, find their fulfillment in him and are permeated by his presence, even when the authors do not use his name. There are some texts in which his voice is stronger than others, but the Lion of Judah prowls through every page of the Bible, and no matter where we turn to we can gather our voices with John the Baptist and proclaim, "Behold the Lamb of God!"

LISTENING TO THE BIBLE

All language begins as spoken language. The written word came eons after the spoken word, and reading came millennia after listening. It is always a derivative form of communication. The words contained in the Scriptures were heard before they were read: prophets, lawgivers, poets, bards, historians and preachers addressing a live audience. The letters of the apostles were read aloud to their recipients who were gathered to listen and eat at the Lord's table. The words were animated by a living voice, carried along by inflection, tone and emotion.

Eugene Peterson calls the written word the "dehydrated" form of the spoken word—two-dimensional and drained of its interpersonal fullness. When we open the Bible we must do so in faith that God has the power to resurrect dead letters.[6] As Scot McKnight says, "What we are looking for in reading the Bible is the ability to turn the two-dimensional words on paper into a three-dimensional encounter with God."[7] It is nothing short of a miracle when, in what amounts to sorting through ancient mail, my world is addressed, my language spoken, my name called.

It signaled a big shift in my approach to the Bible when I started calling it not "reading" but "listening." In listening to the Bible, I remind myself that behind all the words, there is a voice. I aim to listen to a person before I dissect a text. McKnight calls this a "relational" approach to the Bible, one that "invites us to listen to God speak in the Bible and to engage God as we listen."[8] In such an approach, the *who* questions come to the front as we read verses, chapters and books. A passage should incite questions such as, Who is God? Who am I? Who is the church? Who is Jesus, and who is he making us to be? We don't ignore the how and the what questions, because they are necessary for understanding, but we remember that listening to the Bible is ultimately about listening to God. McKnight puts it this way: "Our relationship to the God of the Bible is to listen to God so we can love him more deeply and love others more completely."[9]

When we approach the words with the intent of listening to the Word, we must conclude that our goal is more than intellectual understanding. We work, pray and wait for understanding, but we do not treat it as the ultimate prize. If we seek more of the Bible, then we must bring more of ourselves to it. The "tools" that we use in interpretation are expanded: we do not require just a concordance and a Bible dictionary but humility, surrender, trust, hope. Along with our minds and our reasoning abilities, we bring our hearts, dreams and imaginations, and all the light and dark parts of our personalities. If we submit the deepest parts of ourselves to our listening, we have reason to believe that God will reveal deep parts of himself to us.

THEMES AND PROPOSITIONS, OR HOW TO KILL THE STORY

A product of the public school system in the intellectual and cultural hub of Burien, Washington, I was, of course, required to read many of the classic works of literature in high school. The centerpiece of those assignments was to uncover the "theme" of each work. We mined the pages of *Moby-Dick*, *To Kill a Mockingbird* and *Great Expectations*, sifting through the dialogue, the characters and the plot until we uncovered that gold nugget of the theme. The central moral lesson of the story became our reading treasure, and when we found it, we knew we then understood the book. Even in my obsessive determination to get straight A's back then, a mildly rebellious question frequently crossed my mind: If we are just reading to find the "theme," then what is the point of the story? Instead of whiling away her hours writing *To Kill a Mockingbird*, why didn't Harper Lee just write a bumper sticker: "Racism is bad and good men stop it"? Racism would have been ended forever!

Back then I understood literature as moral lessons wrapped in story. The story was the glittery packaging that we tore into in order to get to the theme.[10] I have often seen the same interpretive strategies in Bible reading and teaching. Our objective in interpreting a biblical story is to find the principles, the propositions that can be proved true or false, which we can then apply to life.

When we read the story of David and Goliath, for example, we might distill the battle narrative into this little elixir: God sides with the little guy. Such a principle becomes a handy tool that can be applied to any number of obstacles we face in life. This principle is simple, manageable and controllable, and it becomes a master key that can unlock almost any door. It no longer matters where we got the key from or who made the key. The context of the story is no longer necessary once we have extracted the principle; the life context of the reader becomes the priority. We can write the principle out on a flashcard and close the book.

LISTENING IN

What if, instead of trying to drag principles, and God, out of the Scriptures, we sought to be drawn into the Scriptures? I want to find my place in the grand story, not extract out pieces of the story, allowing the big story to rewrite my own story. That is why I am drawn to listening approaches that help us find our way into the Bible and meet the God who is already there. These are methods that emphasize conversation with God, using the words of the Scriptures as starting points for those conversations. In other words, Scripture reading becomes prayer.

Praying the Psalms. One of these biblical listening methods is the ancient tradition of praying the Psalms. This practice has structured the rhythms of monastic communities for seventeen hundred years as men and women have cycled through the Psalms, singing and chanting them day after day, week after week, year after year. The best title I have heard for this practice is "Words from God, Words to God."

Sometimes we have to start with the words of others in order to find our own words. Praying the Psalms is a way of praying the words of others in order to find our own prayer. We enter empathically into the praises, celebrations, laments and agony of the psalmists, taking their experiences and struggles into ourselves and offering our own circumstances, joy and pain to God through those words. In repeating their words I often find myself in direct conversation with the Lord. Even more, praying the Psalms is offering God's own inspired words back to him. If you are one of those people who never know what to say in prayer, there is no better place to start than praying God's very words. Let the God-breathed words form your own prayer.

Prayer of the senses. Another method that emphasizes conversation with God through Scripture is the Ignatian style of Bible reading. Ignatius Loyola, the sixteenth-century founder of the Jesuit order of the Catholic Church, developed a creative style of Bible reading that he called "the prayer of the senses."[11] This is an exercise in the prayerful use of the imagination.

In this approach you plunge yourself right into a Gospel story, directly into first-century Palestine. Employing all your imaginative faculties, you feel the desert heat, smell the dust, see the characters and hear their voices. You are not studying the words of the characters as much as you are trying to enter into their world: you see the lines on their faces, feel their fears, experience the tensions between people and take on their questions as your own. After you have taken in the scene broadly, you enter into conversation with Jesus as though you are a character in the story.

Let's experiment with this. Say you want to enter into the story in Mark 9 where Jesus encounters a father whose son suffers from violent seizures. You pray for openness, and then you shine your imagination on the father's troubled face, the scolding faces of the scribes and the scared faces of the disciples. You smell the sweat of the hot crowd packed in around the boy. You see the poor boy convulsing on the ground, eyes rolled back in his head, the dust swirling around him. You feel his pain and his fear. You hear the gasps of the onlookers. You detect the tremble in his dad's voice when he begs Jesus, "I believe! Help my unbelief!"

Then you see Jesus approach the boy, his face still glowing from his transfiguration on the mountain, and speak with the authority only he has. The boy exhales and his body goes limp, and you are sure that he is dead. But then Jesus takes the boy's hand and raises him off the ground, new life bursting forth. You feel the warmth in their clasped hands and you are pierced with joy and relief as dad and son embrace.

Now, without leaving that dramatic scene, you interact with Jesus. Perhaps there is one character in the story that you most resonate with, and if so, you ask the questions that the experience of that character prompts. If you relate to the father, you might ask, in the presence of Jesus, where in my life do I find faith? Where do I find unbelief and doubt? Or perhaps you sympathize with the son, and you ask, what are my places of pain? What do I fear? How do I need healing and new life? Then listen for Jesus' response. Does he speak? What does he say? Is his tone gentle? Does he correct you? Is he smiling? Does he seem compassionate? How do you feel as you listen?

In an Ignatian reading of a Gospel story, we do not treat our imaginative reconstruction as an extension of Scripture, and we must be careful to weigh anything we hear Jesus say against the balance of the whole biblical witness, community and prayerful discernment. What we imagine in a scene tends to reveal more about us than it does about God, but this is good news because those personal revelations can become grounds for fruitful interactions with the Lord in prayer.

Lectio divina. The practice of *lectio divina* is what resurrected my devotional reading of the Bible. It takes the Bible's inspiration so seriously that it declares every word, every letter and every squiggle has its ultimate origin in God. Those words and characters are not stuck in the past but, because they are enlivened by the Holy Spirit, are means for God's communication with us today. Lectio listens through old words for a new word. A twelfth-century monk with a funny name, Guigo the Second, is credited for the classic formulation of *lectio divina*, which literally means "sacred reading."[12] The core idea is that through your settling into a text and slowly reading through it multiple times, the Holy Spirit may give you a particular word, phrase or idea in that passage that becomes the basis for prayer and reflection. I like to put it this way: in listening to a Scripture you may find that something in it *sings* to you. The words flow in a linear and unsurprising sequence until suddenly a word or phrase leaps out at you, and the angels start singing. This is a clue that God is speaking to you, and you hang on to it for all it's worth. *Lectio divina* lets you stretch out that experience, turning over the word in your mind, listening to it and praying it, and through it being drawn into God's presence.

The four steps in Guigo's approach are in Latin: *lectio* (reading), *meditatio* (meditation), *oratio* (prayer) and *contemplatio* (contemplation). I like to reframe those movements in listening terms.[13]

Listen. Slowly read through the text two times. Read it aloud and enunciate carefully, pausing between sentences. You're reading this like you would a love letter, trying to capture every tone and resonance, the emotions in and around the words, and the pregnant silences in between words and sentences. Take the words into your heart. If anything sings to you, take note without judging or analyzing it.

Ask. Read through the passage again, paying attention again to anything that sings to you. Is there a word or phrase that stands out? Something that seems mysterious or attractive and holds your attention? If so, spend time with it. Reflect on it and why it seems important. This isn't time for intellectual exercise or reading commentaries but for personal reflection. How does it speak to your life? Is there an invitation in it?

Answer. Read through it one more time, praying the words. Now interact with the Lord through what you have read. If a word or phrase sang to you, ask for understanding. If an invitation emerged, offer it to God and listen for his response. If a relationship, struggle or dark part of your life surfaced, do not hold that back. Be as honest as possible, knowing that the Lord searches our hearts and knows us better than we know ourselves. Is there a fresh word that he is speaking to you right now?

Be. The words of the Scriptures are windows intended to bring us face to face with the Word behind them. In this last phase, linger in the presence of the Lord. Let the word you have heard sweep you up into his embrace. Sit in silence, enjoying him and being with him without feeling pressure to speak or do anything. Let God sing his song over you.

The practice of *lectio divina* reminds us that we are never done listening to the Scriptures because God is never done speaking to us through them. Just like we can savor a classic piece of music over and over, listening for all the parts and layers and lines of instrumentation, hearing something new each time, we can return again and again to a passage of Scripture because its richness and beauty is never exhausted and because God shows us new things and speaks fresh words to us each time. Then we can take what we have heard and carry it with us all day, a song we want stuck in our heads, playing and replaying and reminding us of Immanuel, God with us.

THE CHARACTER OF THE LISTENER

A listening approach to the Bible is deeply personal. It does not preclude other forms of reading, but it acknowledges that the best kind of Bible reading happens when our minds are swept up into the presence of God and our hearts kindled by what we hear. For that reason, I am fascinated by how the church fathers of the fourth and fifth centuries understood biblical interpretation. They refused to separate intellectual pursuit from spiritual pursuit, instead insisting that the most important component in good Bible reading is the character of the listener.

Professor Christopher Hall explains that "the fathers considered the Bible a holy book that opened itself to those who themselves were progressing in holiness through the grace and power of the Spirit. The character of the exegete would determine in many ways what was seen or heard in the text itself." For example, the third-century bishop Athanasius proclaimed that "the searching and right understanding of the Scriptures [demands] a good life and a pure soul. . . . One cannot possibly understand the teachings of the saints unless one has a pure mind and is truly to imitate their life."[14]

The fathers would claim that our lack of understanding comes from our refusal to live what we read. It is not that our minds are empty; it is that our hearts are closed. This echoes what Jesus himself said: "Anyone who resolves to do the will of God will know whether the teaching is from God or whether I am speaking on my own" (John 7:17). A commitment to act on what we hear is what authenticates the truth of Jesus' words. We do not understand because we do not obey. As Eugene Peterson puts it, "The most important question we ask of the text is not, 'What does this mean?' but 'What can I obey?' A simple act of obedience will open our lives to this text far more quickly than any number of Bible studies and dictionaries and concordances."[15]

Wisdom is given along the way of obedience. To declare that the Bible is inspired is not the same thing as living a life inspired by the Bible. When we aim not only to read the Law, the Prophets and the letters but to become "letters of Christ," "known and read by all" (2 Corinthians 3:2-3), then we will be given access to the meaning of the Scriptures. We must be willing to listen, even when it's hard. We can labor on an intellectual level to understand what Jesus means when he says forgive "not seven times, but . . . seventy-seven times" (Matthew 18:22), but until we actually seek to forgive the person who has hurt us deeply, we are not truly listening to the Scriptures.

CONCLUSION: IMPROVISING THE SCRIPTURES

We know we have listened well to the Scriptures when afterward we are summoned to play. We are not soothed into sleep by the Bible, a pleasant lullaby, but we are jolted awake and summoned to take what we have heard and improvise on it with our lives.

Many years ago I played alto saxophone in the high school jazz band, which met in the "zero hour." I have bittersweet memories of driving through dark and misty Seattle mornings to the music room, where a half-awake group of teenagers tried to jam, as much as white suburban kids are capable. I was skilled at playing notes when they were written out for us, but when it came to improvisation, I was a disaster. Improvising is taking the chords you are given, the base line that accompanies you, your imagination and your courage, and creating something new, your own composition. When I tried to improvise I either played a chaotic and random set of notes or else I parroted what the person before me had played.

The ideal of improvisation is that you create something new, but within the musical boundaries that have been set. You do not quote verbatim what has come before, but you do not play random chaos either. You can stretch and push the boundaries, but your solo has to make sense within the piece. This is not a free-for-all with no rules or boundaries, a scattered group of teenagers fiddling with their instruments. This is why the best improvisers are also the best listeners. Spend time in a jazz club and you'll notice that during a solo the other members of the band are listening, because they know that when their turn comes they can create something new, but it must be coherent with what has come before. It has to flow.

Our call is to listen to the Bible, particularly the Christ story that weaves through its pages, and then to improvise with what we have been given. We gauge our listening abilities by how well and how faithfully we play. We don't listen just to be filled with knowledge, and we don't treat the Scriptures only as sheet music that we endlessly rehearse and memorize. The big movements of the Scriptures are the chords and rhythms that drive us forward into our own faithful and inventive compositions. Our improvisation flows from what we have heard, and with the Scriptures ringing in our ears, we move forward to create something new and stirring, a piece that is compelling to those who listen to us.

FIVE

Listening to Creation

IT IS UNLIKELY THAT THE TERM "mountain man" will appear in my obituary. John Muir's beard would survive longer in the wilderness than I would. Once, during a blustery storm in the Sierras, Muir shimmied to the top of a tall Douglas fir to experience what it feels like to be a tree in gale-force winds. To rival that, the last time I went camping I probed so deep into the forest that there were only two bars of reception left on my cell phone. In my defense, I grew up in the Northwest, and I was warned not to go far into the woods because Bigfoot would eat me.

When I get together with my college friends, they like to tell the story of the toothbrush. A few years back we all went camping in the Angeles National Forest, in the mountains above Los Angeles. I think it was the second camping trip of my life. Most of the group had retired to their tents after dinner, when my friend Darcy, from within her tent, called out with some alarm, "What is that sound?" My other tented friends chimed in: "Is that an engine? Is there a car here? What is going on?" Standing outside in the dark, I looked around and shrugged, "No, there's no one here. What are you hearing?" "It's some kind of whirring noise that sounds like a motor," explained Sean, my college roommate. "Oh," I mumbled, "that's my toothbrush." I never got the memo stipulating that standard camping gear does not include an electric toothbrush.

When I write a chapter about creation, I am not doing so as a naturalist or as a modern-day Saint Francis. There are no squirrels or birds perched on my shoulders as I write this. I am closer to Homer Simpson, who, in imagining himself following in the footsteps of Thoreau to move into the woods and keep a record of his thoughts, writes his first journal entry: "I wish I'd brought a TV. Oh God how I miss TV."

My entry into this topic did not happen while swooning over a 360-degree vista on a mountain peak or while tracing my finger along a somber autumn leaf. I became open to the power and wonder of a world out there while reading a book indoors. An ancient book that says things like:

When I look at your heavens, the work of your fingers,
    the moon and the stars that you have established;
what are human beings that you are mindful of them,
    mortals that you care for them? (Psalm 8:3-4)

The voice of the LORD is over the waters;
    the God of glory thunders,
    the LORD, over mighty waters.
The voice of the LORD is powerful;
    the voice of the LORD is full of majesty.

The voice of the LORD breaks the cedars;
    the LORD breaks the cedars of Lebanon.
He makes Lebanon skip like a calf,
    and Sirion like a young wild ox.

The voice of the LORD flashes forth flames of fire.
The voice of the LORD shakes the wilderness;

the LORD shakes the wilderness of Kadesh.

The voice of the LORD causes the oaks to whirl,
    and strips the forest bare;
    and in his temple all say, "Glory!" (Psalm 29:3-9)

Lift up your eyes on high and see:
    Who created these?
He who brings out their host and numbers them,
    calling them all by name;
because he is great in strength,
    mighty in power,
    not one is missing. (Isaiah 40:26)

Look at the birds of the air; they neither sow nor reap nor gather into barns, and yet your heavenly Father feeds them. Are you not of more value than they? And can any of you by worrying add a single hour to your span of life? And why do you worry about clothing? Consider the lilies of the field, how they grow; they neither toil nor spin, yet I tell you, even Solomon in all his glory was not clothed like one of these. But if God so clothes the grass of the field, which is alive today and tomorrow is thrown into the oven, will he not much more clothe you—you of little faith? (Matthew 6:26-30)

For what can be known about God is plain to them, because God has shown it to them. Ever since the creation of the world his eternal power and divine nature, invisible though they are, have been understood and seen through the things he has made. (Romans 1:19-20)

The more I lingered over texts such as these, the more restless I became with pursuing God only in written words, and the more I suspected he had still more to say to me. The Scriptures do not finally point to themselves, but instead direct us to a Creator, Redeemer and Sustainer who is present and active in the everyday, and who, to paraphrase Abraham Kuyper, surveys every plot of the universe and rightfully declares "Mine!"

I had met the God who is a master wordsmith; I was less familiar with the God who is the master craftsman of each square foot of heaven and earth. Then I stumbled on the ancient Celtic tradition that presents not one but two sacred texts to study: the Bible and what they called "the Big Book," the creation. I have shelves and stacks of theology books in my apartment, yet that moment revealed a creation-sized hole in my library. Saint Bernard of Clairvaux taught that "you will find something more in woods than in books. Trees and stones will teach you that which you can never learn from the masters."[1] Whereas books usually speak in prose, the creation speaks in poetry. If we take the time to listen, we may discover that we are surrounded by parables and allegories and lyrics that defy the skill of our most touched poets.

My theology gave me a lofty excuse for being unimpressed with the artistry surrounding me. I am revealing my Reformed tendencies here when I say I believe the rebellious human heart is bent toward idolatry. We are inclined to take anything that is good and make it too good, turning creatures into gods that we worship. Yes, the apostle Paul says that the nature of God is revealed in the ways of creation in Romans 1, but two chapters later he chains us all to the shackles of sin and its power to distort our minds and hearts. We may have been born to praise the Creator through his creatures, but now we find ourselves praising the creatures and forgetting about, or remaking, the Creator. These are the roots of pantheism—believing that everything is God—or panentheism—believing that

God is *in* everything. In my determination not to careen down these slopes, I kept my eyes to the ground and my ears closed to the everyday miracles around me.

But if I use theology to shield me from delighting in God's works and hearing his voice through them, then something is dreadfully askew with the way I do theology. We can't let others who don't share our beliefs have a deeper experience of nature than we do because we are afraid of heresy. It is true that God's essence will not be found in that rock by the path, but it is also true that if we don't cry out in praise, then the stones will. No one should exult in creation like Christians and no one should stand guard over the environment like Christians, because we have met the King of creation and his thrones are scattered everywhere.

While I agree with John Calvin when he says that "it is fitting that he prick up his ears to the Word, the better to profit,"[2] I also thrill when he says, "Meanwhile let us not be ashamed to take pious delight in the works of God open and manifest in this most beautiful theater."[3] As our hearts and minds are renewed inwardly through hearing the gospel, all our senses are restored and we are able to clearly experience God's movements in the world outside of us. We live in the era of new creation, inaugurated when a man walked out of a tomb on Sunday morning, squinting while his eyes adjusted to the sun rising on the new week. In this new creation, humans are being restored to the original purpose for which they were created, and the creation itself is being renewed to do what it was designed to do—namely, point people to the God who prepared the worlds by his word, making what is visible out of what is invisible.

LISTENING FOR THE SECRET OF CREATION

The world God makes and the word God speaks are working together to reveal creation's great secret.[4] By itself creation offers at best a general direction toward a Creator, but the Word gives us coordinates.[5] We are given hints at the secret in the Old Testament, in God's creating word of Genesis and in the personified wisdom of Proverbs, but we do not fully learn the secret until the opening pages of the New Testament. The guidance of the stars and the prediction of the prophets, the world and word, led the philosophers of the East to Bethlehem, where they learned that the closely guarded secret of creation is not information but a person, Jesus Christ. Before that moment he was the uncredited actor of creation, but from this point on we do not understand creation unless we realize it was made through Christ and for Christ. He is creation's source, its means and its goal. He is the Logos, the wisdom through which the world was made and the one in which everything hangs together. He is the meeting place of word and world.

Once the secret of creation has been whispered to us, it unlocks everything. When we understand that God is supremely in Jesus Christ, we start to hear echoes of his voice everywhere. Creation has been given a face and a personality. We will then realize that from our first breath, creation has been teaching us about grace. Behind all matter, there is a mind. Behind the beauty of the world, there is wisdom. Behind the playfulness and delight that fills creation, there is love. N. T. Wright calls the creation a "signpost," faithfully pointing us toward the Creator and toward the day when heaven and earth will stage the can't-miss wedding event of the ages. All the glories and miracles and wonders of creation are a drum roll building toward the full unveiling of Jesus Christ, when the secret will be shouted from the highest mountains and in the depths of the seas.

THE SOUND THE UNIVERSE MAKES

We know the universe through light. What we can observe is dependent on the illumination of the sun and the stars. But the universe is not silent. The psalmist announced this three thousand years ago:

> The heavens are telling the glory of God;
>> and the firmament proclaims his handiwork.
> Day to day pours forth speech,
>> and night to night declares knowledge.
> There is no speech, nor are there words;
>> their voice is not heard;
> yet their voice goes out through all the earth,
>> and their words to the end of the world. (Psalm 19:1-4)

This psalm introduces us to a universe that *preaches*. Creation is not only a banquet for the eyes, but it speaks messages to our inner ears. There are no audible words, yet the cosmic pulpit preaches the most powerful and well-crafted homilies you'll ever hear. Creation is alive, and it is talkative. Messages sound in the skies and are recorded on the earth, not as superstitions or horoscopes, because they speak in unison. Saint Augustine heard the message in the fourth century:

> But what is my God? I put my question to the earth. It answered, "I am not God," and all things on earth declared the same. I asked the sea and the chasms of the deep and the living things that creep in them, but they answered, "We are not your God. Seek what is above us." I spoke to the winds that blow, and the whole air and all that lives in it replied. . . . I am not God." I asked the sky, the sun, the moon, and the stars, but they told me, "Neither are we the

God whom you seek." I spoke to all the things that are about me, all that can be admitted by the door of the senses, and I said, "Since you are not my God, tell me about him. Tell me something of my God." Clear and loud they answered, "God is he who made us."[6]

The heavens, the earth and the seas are devoted and faithful preachers because all they do is sing the praises of the One who created them. They stand tirelessly in their ancient pulpits testifying to the raw power, the exquisite beauty, the tender mercy and the playful creativity of their Maker. Even inanimate objects soundlessly give witness to the one who breathed life into the world and who sustains it moment by moment.

God spoke creation into existence, and now creation speaks of his existence. The world was formed by God's word, so we should not be surprised that just like his word, his world restores, nourishes, inspires, teaches, exhorts, surprises, disrupts, moves and comforts us. Because creation is born of God's speech, all our exploration and hikes and study and enjoyment of nature is an act of sacred listening. Creation may first present itself to us as art for the eyes, and we are grateful that the Artist chose a palette dripping with color and light and wonder, but slowly we can come to understand that creation is also a feast for our spiritual ears as we make ourselves available to the messages God whispers through it.

CREATION'S SERMON

If Thoreau went into the woods to live deliberately, then I plunged myself into God's world to listen deliberately. I wanted to avail myself of creation's pulpit, to sit in rocky and sandy and grassy chapels that I might hear their sermons. As Richard Foster puts it,

I wanted to study the book of nature to discover what the Lord might teach.[7]

Something else drove me out into the wilderness: exhaustion. If you think you get tired of hearing your pastor preach, then imagine how tired your pastor gets of hearing himself preach. Being a pastor is a noble calling, yes, but it can also be a soul-draining one. On some days the bride of Christ seems more like the bride of Frankenstein. I know that human beings are the pinnacle of creation and that our fullest experiences with creation involve community. Feeling closer to God in nature than in church is an authentic feeling but not ultimately full biblical spirituality. Yet there is something healing about retreating into nature when the church has worn you out. Creation praises God even when I can't. John Muir, who was hurt by the church early in his life but found therapy in the solitude of nature, said that "everybody needs beauty as well as bread, places to play in and pray in where nature may heal and cheer and give strength to the body and soul."[8] Centuries earlier, Saint Francis used to walk in the fields and preach the gospel to flowers and animals. I am more inclined to let the flowers and animals preach to me. Unlike my sermons, theirs never get boring.

A WATERFALL SANCTUARY

The good news, especially for less-than-adventurous types like me, is that creation surrounds us. We don't have to retrace Lewis and Clark's route in order to receive creation's counsel. For ten years I lived in an apartment at the foothills of the San Gabriel mountain range of Southern California, and for a few days in the winter my writing desk looked out through a line of palm trees at snow-sprinkled hills. From the angle of my view, the smaller peaks shrouded the grandfather of the San Gabriel range, Mt. Baldy, so named because of the treelessness of his forehead.

In the late weeks of summer, when the sun was wreaking its last revenge, Grandpa Baldy called to me from his hiding place. The desert heat made it all but impossible to venture outside during daylight hours, and I was a prisoner to air conditioning. I would get restless. One summer, the perennial restlessness set in, but that time it was encouraged by anxiety I was feeling about the future and whether any of my big dreams would ever intersect with reality. My restless energy needed to move, so I got in my car and drove to San Antonio Falls, which sits two-thirds of the way up to Baldy's widow's peak.

I'm convinced Jesus wasn't lost in a moment of whimsy when he gestured toward the fields seeded with life and color and told his disciples to "consider the lilies of the field, how they grow; they neither toil nor spin, yet I tell you, even Solomon in all his glory was not clothed like one of these. But if God so clothes the grass of the field, which is alive today and tomorrow is thrown into the oven, will he not much more clothe you?" (Matthew 6:28-30). He knew that one of the best ways to combat anxiety, and its cruel whispers about scarcity, is to immerse yourself in the super-abundance of creation. Somehow the promise of a "peace beyond understanding" is more real when I ask for it while sitting on a mountain or along a body of water. Creation is full of gifts given just because, not as a reward or payment for work. Lilies grow just because. Waterfalls flow because they can. Ducks paddle and cackle because that's what they do. They care nothing for my worries. They live in a big world, and mine is small.

San Antonio Falls runs through the middle of a granite channel carved into sheer cliffs, with big boulders scattered at the base that serve as makeshift pews. It is not a terribly impressive waterfall. The water cascades in a three-tiered system, falling straight down and pooling on a level like a ladle, and then plunging down again, and then a final time. I call it "Trinity Falls," splashing down to eternal life. There is a shape at the top that resembles the elongated head and twisting neck of a prehistoric serpent who tempts you not to trust. But the granite adversary has no power to stop the relentless grace and refreshment of Trinity Falls, nor to keep the pool of water at the base from finding its way under the rocks to form the stream below.

I sat there that day on my rocky pew, letting the falls preach to me, asking God to speak in my canyon cathedral. I think I was drawn to Trinity Falls during that season because the plunging falls echoed the restlessness I felt. The ongoing rush of water and sound seemed to sympathize with the energy racing through me. At first its relentless roar underscored my anxiety, but as I continued to sit there, it overtook my anxiousness, slowing it, absorbing it. My mind became quiet, my body exhaled, and I surrendered my anxiety to forces beyond me.

THE SPIRITUAL DISCIPLINE OF THE LONG WALK

Mountain drives may be a luxury of those who live at elevation, but long walks are not. I want to propose the spiritual discipline of the long walk. It is long because the monologue racing through our heads takes a while to talk itself out, and it is a walk because moving any faster would make the world blurry, and this is a practice that is meant to slow us down. It seems that everything I read these days has people talking about "attentiveness." The bullet train of modern life has our landscapes whizzing by, and some of us have decided we need to slow down or get off the train so we don't miss what is right in front of us. We devote too much energy to years and months and hours at the expense of the moment we are currently living. The long walk is about attentiveness, about receiving each moment as a gift and listening to the sermons creation is preaching to us.

The long walk can be practiced anywhere, from a nature walk to an urban neighborhood. The idea behind it is to unplug in order to connect with the Power that surges through the world. I extricate myself from everything, external and internal, that keeps me from being wholly present, and practice a *lectio divina* of the big book of creation.

For the first ten minutes of my walk I am allowing the fog to drift out of my soul, silencing my mind and heart and giving myself over to God's gifts in my immediate surroundings. Then I begin to notice what I see and hear, no matter how big and loud or small and quiet. I'm not trying to insert meaning or concentrate on any one thing; I'm only noticing. Sometimes if I am wearing glasses I will take them off so I can better pay attention to the sounds around me. Unaided, I have the eyesight of an eighty-year-old man with multiple cataracts, so if I take off my glasses I am largely dependent on my hearing. We tend to take in creation mostly through our eyes, but there is a rich symphony being played if we let our ears do some of the work.[9]

Then, after I have perused the book of creation, taking it in on a large scale, I start to pay attention to anything that flashes or sings out at me, something specific that draws me in. If the first stage is taking in the symphony as a whole, now I start to focus in on particular instruments. Is it a lizard lounging on the path? Is it a particular birdcall? Is it the wind shaking the leaves? Is it the shape of a branch in a tree? Is it the chorus of nighttime voices? Whatever it is, study it. Listen to it. What do you see? What do you hear? What seems interesting or significant about it?

There is no pressure for our observations to be theological or spiritual; we are simply waking up to the craftsmanship of God's handiwork around us and listening. There are plenty of lessons to be drawn from the world if we pay attention. Mountains and oceans counsel patience and remind us to slow down. The author of Proverbs thought the ants were worth paying attention to: "Go to the ant, you lazybones; consider its ways, and be wise. Without having any chief or officer or ruler, it prepares its food in summer, and gathers its sustenance in harvest" (Proverbs 6:6-8). Jonathan Edwards found great spiritual meaning in a spider web. He concluded a long letter on the subject this way: "Pardon me if I thought I might at least give you occasion to make better observations on these wondrous animals that should be worthy of communicating to the learned world, from whose glistening webs so much of the wisdom of the Creator shines."[10] Edwards also used the image of a spider suspended over a flame to portray the terrors of coming before a holy God. The guy had a weird thing for spiders.

If taking a walk is a foreign discipline for you, then you have the Bible as a convenient study guide for interpreting our world. A rainbow preaches the covenantal promises and mercy of God. A hen with its chicks reminds us of Jesus' tender care for his people. The wind points to the mysterious work of the Holy Spirit. Rivers echo the justice that will one day cascade down the mountains. The sunrise is a forerunner to resurrection and new creation. Grass and flowers remind us of the fading nature of human life and beauty in contrast to the constancy and permanence of God. A tree takes us into the garden where God gave life in the beginning and takes us to the end when the tree of life will bring the healing of the nations. Raging bears remind us not to mock a prophet's baldness.

If something grabs your attention, carry it in your mind and heart as you walk. Let it preach to you for a while. Allow it to draw you into dialogue with the One who imagined it and made it. Let it roll up into gratitude for the beauty, mercy and wisdom he has surrounded us with. End with "thank you."

CREATION'S SONG

Astronomer Janna Levin explains that black holes, if we could approach and listen to them without being instantly vaporized, make a noise. They spin and curve, stretching and squeezing the space around them, ringing out like a cosmic hand traced around a crystal flute. The dark sky we get lost in during the quiet hours of the night wobbles and beats and resonates like it's powered by astral timpani. Levin says that there is a "sonic composition written on space."[11] The universe is scored.

This may be a new discovery to modern astronomy, but people have been dancing to creation's tune since ancient times. The first chapter of the Bible, the beginning of the heavens and the earth, sounds best when we hear it set to music. The literary structure has rhythm and tempo, a beat that bumps through the passage. There is a cadence to the verses, held together by the refrains repeated on each day of creation: "And God said" and "There was morning and evening, the __ day." On each day a new instrument of creation is introduced, adding a new sound, filling out what has come before, slowly building toward the climactic moment, the fortissimo of creation's symphony: humans made in the image of God.

The lyrics of the creation song establish clear rhythms:

There are 6 days of work and then 1 day of rest. Six days and a sabbath. The weeks of the year go: 6 and 1, 6 and 1, 6 and 1. As Rob Bell puts it, "God is the God of the groove."[12]

Eugene Peterson breaks down the music further, pointing out that God performs *one* creative action on the first, second, fourth and fifth days of creation. But on the third and sixth days, he performs *two* different acts. On the sixth day, for example, he creates (1) animals to roam the earth and (2) humans to fill and rule the earth. Then on the last day of creation, the sabbath, the number of the day (7) is repeated three times. On the other six days, the number of the day is only noted once. If you bring all these numbers together, you get a pattern of 1 2 3 / 3 4 5 6 / 6 and then 777. In modern music we play to rhythms of 4/4 time or 6/8 time, but perhaps in the ancient Hebrew world the people of God got down to this beat: one, two, three and three, four, five, six and six, seven, seven, SEVEN![13]

I like to think of God approaching the primal watery chaos of non-creation like a world-class conductor walking into a fifth-grade band room. Chaos is the sound of all instruments blaring at once: the teeth-rattling cacophony that comes from untrained and undisciplined novices blowing on their horns and fiddling on the keys just to see what sound they can make. The capricious gods of neighboring societies thrived on this sort of discord, making the world out of their own violence and conflict. The Hebrew God heard the chaos and responded by writing a piece of music so melodic and beautiful that the whole cosmos got up and danced to it. And the Maestro played it again and again until the powers of chaos were worn out.

It is as if God was able to write his triumphal song directly onto the surface of creation itself. We find ourselves in a world that is not static, but pulsates with the ongoing rhythms of morning and evening, sunrise and moonrise, cloud cover and cloud break, waxing and waning, waking and sleeping, work and rest, autumn and winter, dormancy and bud burst, seedtime and harvest. And the creation beat goes on and on.

Every morning we wake up to a song we did not write,[14] a reveille that rousts us from our sleep and gets us moving. When our feet first touch the ground, we step into an ongoing dance, and none of us is put there to be a wallflower. Human life is designed to be lived rhythmically, in step with the innate rhythms of creation. When we try to stand over creation, instead of acting as participants in it, we ignore its natural rhythms and time crashes into itself: hours and days and weeks flow into one another, and we begin to lose track of when one thing starts and another ends. Without separation and demarcation our lives alarmingly start to resemble the amorphous blob of chaos that God sang into submission. Humans may be the crowning jewel of creation, but we are not sovereign over it. True freedom comes not from trying to control life's rhythms but from moving in harmony with them.

SLEEP

Our technological innovations, beginning with the light bulb, have enabled us to isolate ourselves from the rhythms that our ancestors had no other option but to live by.[15] We have inverted light and dark; if we choose, we can work all night and sleep all day. It seems that the whole of the Western world has become a colossal city that never sleeps. This takes a physical toll: study after study has revealed an epidemic of sleep deprivation in this country, and lack of sleep is a leading cause of car accidents as well as a contributing factor to conditions such as diabetes and obesity.

Our cultural drowsiness also extracts a subtler, and more insidious, spiritual toll. There is something God defying about refusing to let our bodies get the sleep they need and relentlessly choosing activity over rest. It is no coincidence that the first day after the creation of human beings in Genesis is the sabbath. Men and women were charged with the commission to work the land and fill the earth, and then, as they marshaled their energy for such an enormous task, the sun rose on a day of . . . rest. Sabbath is the grand anticlimax of a week's work. It is a clear message that the world does not ultimately belong to us. No amount of our labor or activity will keep it turning on its axis. God never slumbers or sleeps, but to be human is to sleep, and sleep is a profound gift of rest, release and detachment. "I will both lie down and sleep in peace; for you alone, O Lord, make me lie down in safety" (Psalm 4:8).

Not only does sleep restore our bodies and minds, it reminds us that the world, for eight hours every single day, somehow manages without us. It is not waiting anxiously for us to kickstart it in the morning. We can rest in the knowledge that even while we're dead to the world, the beat goes on.

SEASONS

In Southern California seasons are largely a state of mind. Annual weather patterns here follow the retail calendar: we have summer, and we have Christmas. If you close your eyes and point to any day of any month, odds are it will be sunny, blue and warm. I have been trying to land a gig as a weather forecaster in Los Angeles for years.

Our weather patterns are marked by uniformity, and as a result, our lifestyles often are as well. Rob Bell observes that "when the weather is the same year-round, you tend to live at the same pace year-round."[16] When the weather neglects to take its cues from seasonal shifts, so do we. Unfortunately, when you continuously move at the same speed and engage in the same activities, you often find yourself exhausted, restless and bored.

What if, instead of trying to transcend the rhythms of the calendar, we took guidance from them? I'm not necessarily suggesting that you strip down and howl at the next full moon. But the drama that plays out in the skies above us so often parallels and even affects the drama that acts in us. Perhaps the seasons are a lesson-book for the soul, instructing us when to move fast and when to slow down, when to act and when to rest, when to focus on the world outside and when to hibernate and go down deep.

I love that the word *deciduous* has the word *decide* embedded in it. I like to think that certain trees "decide" to shed their leaves annually, like they're tired of giving so much energy to their leaves and need a change. Even though I live in an ever-green climate, I have resolved to lead a deciduous life. I am determined to listen to the seasons and to receive their instruction, even if where I live they are subtle teachers.

I once lived an hour and a half inland in Southern California, which made for slightly cooler winters and summers that would make Dante blush. If you cracked an egg on the sidewalk at high noon in August, it turned into a chicken. But what I appreciate about living in a climate with minimal variation is that it forces me to pay attention to the nuances of the seasonal shifts. Summer does change into fall, but you have to carefully investigate the shift. I have slowly trained myself to notice the low cloud cover that flirts with the mountains in September. The air warms up just a little slower in the morning and cools down a little faster in the afternoon. The arc of the sun starts to resemble more of an inverted smirk than a broad smile. The light falls differently and casts longer shadows; the loud pink rays of the summer sunset are brushed aside by the soft amber and burnt orange hues of fall's curtain.

I am also learning to notice the equally subtle emotional changes that accompany the seasonal transitions. I think Leighton Ford is on the mark when he asks, "Isn't it true that we usually think of the seasons less in terms of dates that begin and end than in terms of their effect on us: the cold of winter, the awakening of spring, the glow of summer, the pathos of autumn leaves?"[17] For me fall is a season of exhilarating sadness, a time when we marvel at radiant colors and celebrate harvest yet mourn the inevitable retreat of the world back into the ground. Winter is a contemplative season, a time for gratefully reflecting on what has come before and quietly hoping for what is coming. Spring blossoms with renewal and romance and resurrection. Summer is a time of openness, abundance and relaxation, when the living is easy.

In noticing the patterns of fluctuation around us, we are given permission to embrace the changes and varied responses in our souls and bodies. We don't need to fight them. The seasons relieve us from the pressure to put on the same face and act the same way all year round. It's not always summer, and we don't need to live and feel like it is. Just as our wardrobes change for the seasons, so do our emotional and spiritual lives. We can cycle through our own seasons of dormancy and new life, activity and quietness, celebration and sadness, blossom and harvest, openness and being closed, austerity and abundance.

Perhaps we can think of the rhythms of creation as our dance partner. If you try to dance the samba the entire time, you will burn out and end up exhausted and sore. Sometimes you need to slow down and dance the waltz. Sometimes you need to just stand there and sway a little bit. Every few songs you need to sit one out. Winter gives us the opportunity to go dormant for a while; spring invites us to speed up and get to work. All of the seasons offer us a different pace, different activities and different ways to respond to the life of God in us.

We can also allow the rhythms of the days and the seasons to shape our lives of prayer, adding our voices to creation's ongoing and unstoppable chorus of praise. Important wings of the church have been praying with creation for centuries. It is the foundation of the daily office, the regular intervals of prayer offered by communities of believers stretching all the way back to ancient Judaism and early Christianity.[18] This structured form of prayer, also called praying the hours, was perfected in medieval monasteries, where initiates would gather five to seven times per day, at sunrise, high noon, midday, sunset and bedtime, to sing the Psalms, repeat scripted prayers and offer intercession for the world. The practice of prayer interwoven with the work, meals and leisure of an ordinary day is a way of acknowledging God's continual presence in all of life. Each hour of the day, as it turns over from the previous hour and counts down to the next one, is the domain of the Lord, and therefore all of life is a rhythmic offering of our activities, attitudes and rest to him.

I like to think of praying the hours as keeping watch for the Lord, like a guard in an ancient watchtower, eagerly waiting for the dawn to overtake the blackness. In setting aside specific times for prayer, we are keeping watch for the Lord's movements throughout the day. We are not beholden to the rare moments of spontaneous praise, intercession or cries for help, but we follow regular and repeated patterns, the tick tock of the praying life. The Lord wakes us up in the morning, calls us to work, blesses and provides for our meals, and guards our sleep. We acknowledge he is present in the hope of sunrise, the glow of midday, the bittersweet of sunset and the uncertainty of night. At each hour, we watch and we wait for him.

The broader church calendar also keeps watch over the rhythms of the year, tying together the seasonal and the spiritual. Sometimes the big events on the liturgical calendar move in continuity with the season, and sometimes they work in contrast to the time of the year. The church fathers established December 25 as Christmas Day because it coincided with the winter solstice. The shortest and darkest days of the year were the backdrop for the entrance of the Light of the world into the deep night. The season of Lent, on the other hand, comes from the Latin word for "lengthening," indicating the slow progress of daylight in the winter months. Lent is a somber time of self-examination and repentance, but our hearts slowly lift as the days grow longer and the promise of resurrection draws closer. We spend a season meditating on our internal darkness while the days are slowly flooded with greater light. Henri Nouwen explains that "the season of Lent, during which winter and spring struggle with each other for dominance, helps us in a special way to cry out for God's mercy."[19]

When I consider all the rhythms in creation resonating to the glory of God, I am most entranced by the waxing and waning of the tides. Few spiritual practices are as meaningful to me as sitting on the beach, praying with the movement of the waves. I learned recently that this is part of a tradition called "praying with the elements," in which we let the basic components of creation—earth, wind, water and fire—draw us into prayer.[20] Like me, my friend Lara is drawn to water, and she finds that surfing is an act of worship for her. As she puts it, "When you are in the ocean you quickly realize that you cannot conquer it. It's too powerful. If you fight it, you will lose. But if you are skilled enough, what you can do is move in rhythm with it. It's just like God. You will never overpower God, no matter how hard you fight, but you can learn how to move in harmony with him."

I have an irrationally intense fear of jellyfish, so I prefer to stay on the beach rather than surf. I sit in the sand at dusk, and I pray according to what Ignatius of Loyola called the consolations and desolations of God. As the waves crash I inhale the salt air and receive the Lord's consolations: his mercy, goodness and presence. As the waves flee I exhale, and I release the desolations, the places of my life where God does not seem present and the parts of my interior life that I do not want.

CREATION'S GROAN

In the early centuries of the church, new Christians were baptized at dawn on Easter Sunday. After they were plunged into the waters, they would emerge facing east, toward the rising sun that presided over resurrection and new life. As morning prevailed over night, new creation grew one by one.

But sometimes the Easter sunrise service gets rained out. Sometimes the ancient beat gets interrupted. Many of us become aware of creation's rhythms only in these moments, when the music stops and we're left without a chair to sit on. News broadcasts never kick off with "This just in: the sun rose today." It's the hurricanes, earthquakes, floods and fires that get the press. We are never more unsettled than when the things we take for granted stop working, when the cycles that sustain life become forces of death.[21] In those moments we face our vulnerability and temporarily lose the delusion that we have control over our environment.

The songs of creation are not all happy ones. Funeral marches sometimes interrupt parades. We are reminded that something has gone terribly awry with the world every time disaster and death disrupt routine and predictability. C. S. Lewis said that pain is God's megaphone to the world letting us know that something is wrong,[22] and the Bible tells a story not only of human beings in pain but of the entire creation crying out in agony. When we denied our Creator, it disrupted our lives and relationships and also the life and patterns of all creation. It is as if human rebellion caused a shift in the tectonic plates, causing them to crash upon themselves, sending up mountains where there were once plains, collapsing forests into valleys, and the entire world has been experiencing horrendous aftershocks ever since. The ground has been choking on our blood ever since Cain murdered Abel. As Pope John Paul II explained, "When man turns his back on the Creator's plan, he provokes a disorder which has inevitable repercussions on the rest of the created order. If man is not at peace with God, then earth itself cannot be at peace."[23]

Paul says that creation is *groaning* in its enslavement, longing for redemption and freedom. In that language we hear echoes of ancient Israel's travails in Egyptian captivity, and indeed of the human predicament as a whole. In Romans 8 Paul uses the same Greek word to refer to both the groaning of creation and, in the next verse, the groaning of humans as they struggle and wait for salvation.[24] The fates of creation and humanity are intertwined. As goes one, so goes the other. Thus we must listen not only for creation's sermon and creation's song but also for creation's groan. We listen to it because it is also our groan. Creation's story is our story. Made for life, beauty and praise, the natural world has become alienated from its true purpose and now is at war with itself and with us. The dramatic tension plays out before us every day: beauty intermingles with violence, ominous clouds battle with blue skies, comedy overlaps with tragedy, weeds suffocate flowers. We hear the groans of creation every time a fire rages in a national forest, every time a flood washes away everything in its path.

To listen to the groans of creation is to take seriously that we are the source of its pain. Not only did human transgression disrupt the good rhythms that God planted in the world, but our ongoing abuse of creation only enslaves it further. Much of creation reads like a police report of human crimes and greed. There is a broad consensus now that our mistreatment of the environment is contributing to rising temperatures, erratic weather, melting glaciers and the subsequent rise of sea level, erosion of coastlines, more frequent flooding, a decrease in crop yields and topsoil, and broad damage to ecosystems.[25] The creation groans under the weight of widespread pollution and the increase of greenhouse gases that interrupt natural rhythms of airflow.

Sometimes the groans of creation are loud, and sometimes they sound like a cavernous silence. A September 2012 article in *The*

Guardian featured a man who has been recording nature sounds around the world for forty years. Bernie Krause laments that habitats he visited a few years ago, when the waters chattered with animals feeding and playing and bumping against one another, have now fallen silent. Nature's soundtrack is fading away. Extinction of species, shrinking habitats, pollution and human disturbance are irreparably silencing once-noisy ecosystems. Krause writes, "A great silence is spreading over the natural world even as the sound of man is becoming deafening. Little by little the vast orchestra of life, the chorus of the natural world, is in the process of being quietened. There has been a massive decrease in the density and diversity of key vocal creatures, both large and small."[26]

We must also remember that listening to the groans of creation is inseparable from hearing the cries of the poor. It is in poorer countries that the effects of our abuse of creation are most felt. The poor are more affected by climate extremes and natural disasters and have less ability to recover from them. They are more likely to be displaced by floods and famine, and more affected by the conflicts that are often ignited by a lack of resources.

It is not, therefore, out of an abstract ecology that we listen to creation's groan. We listen because we are motivated by love: love for God's world and love for God's people. In love we must ask ourselves the hard questions about how we consume energy and dispose waste, how we build and use space, how we grow and eat, and who and what pays the costs of our relentless drive for profit and growth.

We can keep our ears open to creation's groan because we know pain is not the last chapter in the story. Everything changes when we reframe the context of groaning. Here is where Paul locates the groans:

> For the creation waits with eager longing for the revealing of
> the children of God; for the creation was subjected to futility,
> not of its own will but by the will of the one who subjected
> it, in hope that the creation itself will be set free from its
> bondage to decay and will obtain the freedom of the glory of
> the children of God. We know that the whole creation has
> been *groaning in labor pains* until now; and not only the cre-
> ation, but we ourselves, who have the first fruits of the Spirit,
> groan inwardly while we wait for adoption, the redemption
> of our bodies. (Romans 8:19-23, emphasis added)

These are not deathbed groans, the last words moaned as life slips
away. These are delivery-room groans, sounds of hope and expectation, the agony and struggle that give way to new life.

There is another remarkable detail in the groaning section of
Romans 8. God groans too. The same Greek word used to describe
the groan of creation and humanity is also applied to the Holy
Spirit. "In the same way, the Spirit helps us in our weakness. We
do not know what we ought to pray for, but the Spirit himself
intercedes for us through wordless *groans*" (Romans 8:26 NIV). God
is more than an audience to our groans. He groans along with us,
joining his voice to the delivery-room chorus. He takes on our
story, our enslavement, our yearnings, our death, and makes our
groans his groan on Good Friday. On Easter Sunday, those groans
of despair become shouts of new birth. His blood spilled on the
ground heals not only those who shed blood but the very ground
crying out under its oppression. One day the flowers of new creation will choke out the weeds of the old order.

THE MUSIC OF THE FUTURE

We listen for the groan of creation, sharing its pain, knowing that things have not yet been fully restored. Although all indications are that these are groans of death, we know that somehow these groans are birthing new life. One day the song of new creation will silence the discords of chaos, once and for all, and heaven and nature will sing the praises of the Lord. But the music of the future has already begun, a piece that bursts with the Hebrew ideal of *shalom*, a world of flourishing and abundance and relationship. If we pay attention, we may occasionally hear the melodies of *shalom* that waft backwards into the present and tease us with a future world.

A few years ago a forest fire rampaged in the hills above Santa Barbara, goaded on by the infamous Santa Ana winds. For several days it voraciously consumed trees, homes and public buildings, sending resident animals and people scattering for safety. Much was lost. But even amid the tragedy there were whispers of a future world. Forest rangers sought to save as many animals as they could, but because there was insufficient room to house rescued animals, some had to share cages. In one cage, rangers had no choice but to pair a fawn and a baby bobcat. They feared the worst, but the situation was desperate. The little bobcat, put in the cage second, immediately pounced on the fawn, to play. Natural enemies became fast friends. They played and ate and slept together, and pictures showed the bobcat actually sleeping on top of the fawn at night. They refused to be separated after more cages arrived.

Here is an early realization of prophetic promises, a precursor to Isaiah's better world:

> The wolf shall live with the lamb,
>   the leopard shall lie down with the kid,
> the calf and the lion and the fatling together,
>   and a little child shall lead them.

The cow and the bear shall graze,
>   their young shall lie down together;
>   and the lion shall eat straw like the ox.
The nursing child shall play over the hole of the asp,
>   and the weaned child shall put its hand on the adder's den.
They will not hurt or destroy
>   on all my holy mountain;
for the earth will be full of the knowledge of the LORD
>   as the waters cover the sea. (Isaiah 11:6-9)

For those that have ears to hear, quiet preludes to this future music whisper to us now.

SIX

Listening to Others

I GOT SERIOUS ABOUT LISTENING when I realized I was missing things. Layers of meaning and opportunities for connection were lurking near the surface of my relationships, but I wasn't hearing them, even with those people I loved most. I was skilled at saying wise and empathetic sounding things; I was more skilled at holding people at arm's length. Whenever a conversation turned toward emotions, I started looking for an exit.

My escapes were subconscious. I didn't realize that I was backing away from conversations and from the people who had the courage, or foolishness, to express heartfelt thoughts to me. It wasn't like I was walking out of the room. Well, I suspect that if my heart had legs it might have tried. I considered a moment of pain, crisis or unfiltered emotion an opportunity to impart my insight, to rescue someone from their weakness, to correct distorted thinking, to evaporate the pain. In my mind it was a chance to engage a problem; in truth I was disengaging from the person. I thought I was adding value to the conversation, but I was devaluing the contributions of the other person. Surprisingly, my strategy to fix people never worked. Not once.

A few years later, when asked to record my personal mission statement, I wrote this:

Above all else, I want the people in my life to know that when they come to me, with whatever is on their mind or heart, they will be heard. I am dedicated to hearing the hearts of those around me.[1]

It's unlikely to make the annals of Christian history alongside Saul on the Damascus road or Saint Augustine's "take up and read" moment, but clearly I went through some kind of conversion experience. The friends I have known for decades would like to award me the "Most Improved" trophy, which we all know is a way of saying "You used to be truly awful, but we're not quite as embarrassed to have you on the team anymore." I get the Most Improved Listener trophy. It's a golden ear.

My mentor Donna wouldn't let me get away with ducking out of emotional conversations. We met every Wednesday afternoon, and she drilled this into me: "Stay in the feeling. *Stay* in the feeling. Stay *in* the feeling. Stay in the *feeling*." Donna seized on my tendency to run from feelings, both from the feelings of the people I worked with and from my own. The pattern was unmistakable: every time someone shared a real feeling, I told them, in one way or another, not to feel it. Sometimes I tried to argue them out of the feeling, sometimes I tried to divert it with humor, sometimes I offered up quick reassurance like "Don't worry, I'm sure it will all work out," and at other times I tried to pray the feeling out of them. I was the feelings exorcist.

The way I dealt with the emotions of others was indicative, as it always is, of the way I treated my own emotions. Every time I walked into a potentially emotional conversation, I checked my heart at the door. I had little capacity for entering into the emotional world of others because I was unfamiliar with the terrain of my own emotional world. When that is the case, you will likely have a ministry of *standing over* people rather than *sitting with* them. All the best listening happens when you sit.

I suspect it was not a coincidence that I soon found myself in a ministry that centered on listening. I am not sure what possessed me to say yes to a hospice chaplain job. Someone out there must have prescribed listening as a cure for my soul. Day after day, for four years, I sat at the bedsides of the dying and the grieving, and I also killed the buzz of every party I attended by simply answering the question "What do you do for a living?" All ministries are (or should be) listening ministries, but in a hospice ministry in particular a listening presence is pretty much all you have to offer. It turns out to be quite a bit. Hospice patients have big feelings. My patients had surprisingly little interest in any input I could provide for their situation. Apparently even my level of insight couldn't fix this whole "dying problem." So I listened. And I empathized. And I reflected back emotions. And a few people departed this world in peace. That was when the phrase "I just listened" left my vocabulary forever. Deep listening is too impactful to ever be preceded by *just*.

A LISTENING HEART

You can give a person all the tools for listening, you can teach him all the right techniques, you can introduce him to the fancy words—active listening, mirroring, paraphrasing and repeating, open-ended questions—but a person's listening ability is not determined by the techniques in his arsenal. The law does not have the capacity to give life. It is not my intention, nor my personality, to delineate a whole host of rules for effective listening. I am determined to take the "list" out of listening. We do listening a disservice, I believe, by making it overly mechanical. It doesn't have to be plodding or boring or like eating your lima beans. It can be utterly exhilarating to listen to someone and to see their eyes light up as they discover something new about themselves and feel their emotions validated. It is one of my greatest joys.

The best way to grow as a listener is to spend time around a great listener. I have gained more from being listened to by a seasoned listener than I have from reading dozens of books on the subject. Show me someone who considers listening to be a natural and intuitive activity and I will show you someone who was listened to well when they were a child. Not everyone was lucky enough to have parents who listened to them well, however, and thus many are working out of a listening deficit. So we need to find a listener to imitate. The truth is that we are unlikely to hear unless we have first been heard.

What I am on a quest for is the *heart* of a listener. When the Lord asked King Solomon what he wanted, Solomon asked for what is usually translated as an "understanding heart" or "discerning mind," but in the Hebrew it is literally a "listening heart" (1 Kings 3:9).[2] That is my prayer as well—for a listening heart. The most gifted teacher cannot give you a listening heart. Those who develop a listening heart are those who want to be a particular kind of person. That is why I care less about the *what* of listening and more about the *who*. Who do I have to become in order to have the capacity to listen? Who is the person who makes for a great listener?

It is one thing to season your talking with a little bit of listening, the sugar that makes the medicine go down. But are you truly motivated to learn how to listen to others? There are costs. Character building is always expensive to the ego. Will you listen not just once but time and time again, approaching relationships with the intention of listening first? You can't just flip a switch at the right moment and listen. You can only reliably listen in the moment if you have become a listening sort of person, someone who has developed a listening heart. I want to be a listener, not just someone who occasionally listens.

Getting to that place starts with some honest self-reflection. For what purpose do I enter a conversation? Is it an opportunity to express my opinions, a chance to be heard? Am I seeking attention or adulation? Do I try to entertain or perform for the other person, to convince them that I am likeable or attractive? Am I trying to show others that I'm right and convert them to my way of thinking? Is it a setting for solving a problem? Do I have a rigid agenda? Related to these questions, how do I view the other person in the conversation? Is he a sounding board for my thoughts? Am I the presumed expert and she the novice who needs to learn? A captive audience for my stories? A sparring partner, someone that I am trying to defeat? Someone who will inhale my hot air?

If we are honest, we will likely discover that some of these approaches are at least partially true for all of us. If you are uncertain about your guilt in these areas, ask a trusted friend who tells you the truth, and then you will be less uncertain. And if we dig down deep, we may discover that our approaches to conversations and people stem from some selfishness in our hearts. The opposite of a listening heart is not a talking heart but a selfish heart.

I believe that true listening wars against the entrenched selfishness of the human heart. The listening heart is one that seeks to give, to learn, to welcome, to serve. In a small but real way, listening imitates the self-emptying act of Jesus, who voluntarily released his claims on ruling in order to serve and give his life.[3] The listening heart strives to put away control, all the ways we can manipulate a conversation for our gain. It is able to stop in the middle of a thought and say, "You're right." The heart of a listener is one that submits, that begins to live out Paul's exhortation to "be subject to one another out of reverence for Christ" (Ephesians 5:21). The listening heart seeks to be present, to be focused on something other than itself and to give its attention away.

Trying to fix, judge, rescue or change others are all subtle ways of exerting power over other people. Instead of entering into the world of another person, we try to force them to enter ours. Good listening flips the power dynamic on its head. He who would be the master becomes the servant, and he who would be the captive audience becomes the storyteller.

The who of the listening life is not limited to the listener. As strangely commonsensical as this sounds, we must remind ourselves that we are listening to *people*. Good listening blows away the straw man. People are complex, layered, multifaceted, beautiful, wounded, contradictory, beloved image-bearers of the Creator. They are minds, hearts, souls and bodies, spilling over with dreams, passions, hurts, regrets and fears. As H. Jackson Brown puts it, "Remember that everyone you meet is afraid of something, loves something, and has lost something."[4] Philo of Alexandria is believed to have said, "Be kind, for everyone you meet is fighting a great battle."[5] We ought to tread carefully and gently, and focus on hearing the hearts, not just the words, of people in our lives.

I suggest we make it our aim to listen *to*, not listen *for*. In listening *for*, we are listening like a prosecuting attorney, trying to uncover a hidden motivation, catch the person in a contradiction or find something to confirm our suspicions. We are setting the trap, poised to say "aha!" at any second. To listen for is deconstructive: we are breaking people down into parts. We listen to collect data. We reduce people to issues or categories or positions in a debate. We may view them as problems to be solved, issues to be diagnosed, shortcomings to be corrected. We listen for inroads or openings to spring our thoughts on them. We are in danger of turning people into mere foils for our opinions, their words simply setups for our musings. Dietrich Bonhoeffer writes that "God does not will that I should fashion the other person according to the image that seems good to me, that is, in my own image."[6]

When we listen *to* people, we are embracing them as whole, not fractions, even if they offer only a small part of themselves to us. That small part is attached to big parts, big memories, big stories, big feelings, big losses and big dreams. To listen to is an act of construction: we help people find integration of their various parts. It is an invitation to other people to settle in, be themselves and speak freely. It doesn't matter that their experiences are different from mine, that their background is unfamiliar to me, that they see things differently and hold different views and process emotions differently. They are welcome in my space.

HOW TO BE A BAD LISTENER

If desire is a key to good listening, the root of bad listening is not flawed technique but a lack of motivation. Motivation will cover any number of listening transgressions. At the same time, it will lead a person to hone his listening approach and to identify bad listening patterns in himself. Let's be honest: there is some bad listening going on out there. The bigger problem may be that it's masquerading as good listening. Some people believe they are good listeners when they are not, and other people sometimes wrongly label others as good listeners.

Here are a few of the usual suspects in the ongoing case of bad listening.

- *The one-up.* "You think that's something? Let me tell you about what happened to me last week!" Here the listener sits quietly through the other person's story only to try to trump them with a better, more interesting story. It's a competition more than a conversation.

- *The sleight of hand.* "Uh huh, that's great. But what I really want to talk to you about is . . ." Listening lulls the speaker into a false sense of security so that they don't see the trick coming, namely, what the speaker's agenda is for the conversation.

- *The inspector.* "Didn't you say last week that . . ." The listener asks a series of questions, usually closed-ended questions, in a way that feels like a detective questioning a suspect, trying to lure him into a confession. Listening is the lightning before the thunder, the burning fuse before the boom.

- *The reroute.* "That reminds me of . . ." The listener takes the topic the speaker has addressed and rolls it over, however clumsily, into the topic she wants to talk about or the story she wants to tell. Nothing will stop her from talking about what she came to talk about.

- *The projector.* "I'm totally dealing with the same thing!" The listener projects his problems onto the speaker, and then projects his solutions onto the speaker's problems. The projector sees himself in every conversation.

- *The interrogation.* "What do you think about . . . ? What is your favorite . . . ? Why are you moving to . . . ?" The listener gets wind of the idea that listening is about asking questions, which is good, but then peppers the speaker with them like a game of dodgeball, which is bad. Here we learn that questions, as helpful as they can be, can also be very controlling, and that they can be vehicles for the questioner's agenda.

- *The password.* "Cheese. I had the best cheese at a dinner party with the mayor last week!" The listener sits quietly through the speaker's conversation, but then seizes on one word that she uses, amid a sea of paragraphs, and treats it as a password that unlocks a whole new conversation. The original context has no bearing on where the password takes you. It sounds funny, but it happens more than you might think. The password sentence usually starts with "Speaking of . . ."

- *The hijack.* You have to give the listener credit with this one: at least he's honest and doesn't even pretend to use what the speaker said as a steppingstone. He refrains from speech while the other person talks and then just starts talking about whatever is on his mind, as though they are two deaf ships passing in the night. I'm reminded of a quote I heard once that says most people do not dialogue; they perform a monologue in the presence of another person.

- *The mechanic.* "Here is what you need to do." This person listens like a mechanic listens to a sputtering engine, trying to diagnose the problem so she can fix it. Contrary to popular cultural thinking, both men *and* women are guilty of this one.

- *The bone of contention.* "I disagree with that!" There are an unfortunate number of listeners who listen specifically for what they disagree with. Ask a pastor what people talk to him about after a sermon if you don't believe me. Even if they agree with 99 percent of what a person says, they will pounce on the 1 percent they don't agree with, and in doing so they ignore what is significant to the speaker.

- *The deflector.* "Yeah, but you . . ." This one is a refuge for people who have a hard time receiving criticism, which, let's be honest, is all of us. Someone offers us feedback, so we quickly return the favor without taking the time to absorb what he said.

- *The boomerang question.* "Did you have a good weekend? Because I . . ." Here a person asks a question of another person with the true intention of answering it herself. The question goes out and then boomerangs back. If you know the answer to your own question, you probably shouldn't ask it. Sometimes when I get a boomerang question, I'll respond, "Why don't you just tell me how *your* weekend went?" That usually gets my message across.

The culprits in these bad listening capers would say that their intentions are good. They would say that they sat quietly and let the other person talk before chiming in and therefore they listened successfully. The problem is that silence and listening are *not* the same thing. Listening is not what you do when you don't know what to say. If you are using your silence to dwell on what is happening internally—to listen to your own inner monologue, to come up with more questions, to form a critique or a rebuttal, to prepare your own story or to otherwise focus less on what the other person is communicating and more on your thoughts about what the other person is communicating—then you are not listening well. True listening is an internal matter; only the listener can truly know in a given moment whether they are listening. You can easily play the part of listening without becoming a listener.

The second, and more prominent, problem is that when you have finished refraining from speech, you immediately turn the conversation toward yourself. Your response, story, disagreement, closed-ended question or agenda is, in reality, about you. The quiet you offered, as a result, has the feel of a setup, as though you were simply biding your time until it was your turn to speak. If you are "listening" in such a way that the speaker must make an abrupt shift to listen, you are not doing it right.

PUSHING THE ARROW

Good listening starts with the scandalous premise that this conversation is not about you. Allow me to repeat myself: *this conversation is not about you.* Yet everything in us wants to make it about ourselves. It is an ever-present temptation, even if we are not aware of it. Perhaps especially if we are not aware of it.

It is my aim to simplify the art of listening, the art of not making the conversation about you, as much as possible. Imagine that there is a big arrow hovering over the space between two people engaged in a conversation. It is a very smart, mind-reading arrow, and it swivels to point at whomever the attention in the conversation is focused on. To listen, we remind ourselves, is to pay focused and loving attention on another. So, as the listener in this conversation, your goal is to keep the arrow pointing at the other person for as long as possible. That's it. Push the arrow toward the interests, needs and heart of the other person. Encourage the other person to keep talking, to take an idea further, to go deeper into a story, memory or emotion. Then you're listening. If you remember nothing else from this chapter, remember this.

The problem with this arrow is that its gravitational pull is relentlessly in your direction. Just like a compass points due north, the arrow's place of rest is over you. It *wants* to point at you, so that even when it is centered over the other person, it quivers, trying to return home. A good listener, therefore, must be ruthless in pushing the arrow in the direction of other person. During the course of a conversation you must swing it not once but repeatedly away from you.

The core question of a listening conversation is, then, how can I keep the arrow pointed at the other person? The best way to push the arrow is through asking good, open-ended questions. An open question is one that does not have a yes or no answer;

those questions are called closed-ended questions.

Closed question: Did you have a good weekend? [Possible answers: "Yes" or "No."]

Open question: How was your weekend? [Possible answers: "It was incredible because we catapulted over . . ." Or "It was terrible because this huge dragon . . ."]

Though useful for gathering and confirming information, a closed question has a way of limiting the conversation. It leaves the speaker with nowhere to go, and it twirls the arrow right back on the listener after it has been answered. An open question is an invitation, welcoming discussion and elaboration from the speaker. A good open question is gracious and curious, without a hint of control or agenda. Rather than binding like a closed question, it gives the speaker the freedom to answer however she wants, or to not answer at all. An open question will get a person talking about himself, and if I've learned anything about listening, it's that people like to talk about themselves. Get even a shy person talking about himself and you will be in for a long conversation.

A lot of people are good at asking the first question. However, it's the *second* question that often unlocks the conversation. Most people are accustomed to the conversational pattern of back and forth, the talking tennis match, and so after they are finished speaking, they expect the other person to begin. But what if you take what they have said and offer a follow-up question? They are taken off guard, the standard pattern is interrupted and the real listening can begin. An unexpected question, asked at the right time, can open a whole world. The pace of the conversation at this point will often slow down, as the speaker realizes that you care about what she is saying and that you won't interject if she pauses to think or speaks slowly. She will start to trust that you are not just awaiting your turn to speak.

It is deceivingly simple, but I know of no better second question than "Can you tell me more about that?" You adjust it to fit the context and the topic, but that is its essence. Your wife comes home after a bad day, and after she shares why, instead of immediately talking about your day you can ask, "Tell me more. Why did that interaction bother you so much?" Your son gets in trouble at school, and instead of immediately scolding him ask, in a non-shaming way, "How were you feeling when you did that?" If a person has a story to tell, a grievance to air, an idea to share, a confession to make, an emotion to vent or a secret to tell, a good listener will say, "Tell me more."

A second way to push the arrow back toward the speaker is by reflecting back what you have heard. This one always seems to show up in marriage counseling sessions, especially for couples who have been talking past one another for years. The wooden example sounds like this:

> **Speaker:** I am upset that you won't even take the garbage out when I cook dinner and clean up the kitchen afterward. I don't feel like you value the contributions that I make.

> **Listener:** What I am hearing you say is that you don't feel valued for what you do around the house, and you feel that way when I won't take out the garbage.

Let's be honest: too many conversations like that one could drain the love out of any relationship. As someone who has sat through a few of these counseling sessions, I'll confess that reflecting back and paraphrasing what the other person says too many times makes me want to jump out the window. But its point is to short-circuit the defensive response and to keep the attention focused on the speaker. Instead of being dismissive or adversarial, the listener pauses to notice what the person has said and what emotions are behind the statement. He keeps the arrow pointed at her.

In the course of everyday conversation, reflecting back what you hear doesn't have to be so mechanical. Say your husband goes on a rant about how his boss is micromanaging him at work. You keep the arrow pointed at him by saying, in an empathetic way, "It sounds like you're feeling angry and controlled at work these days," and then pause. You're not simply summarizing what he has said, as though you're writing a book report on his side of the conversation. You're bringing your own mind, heart and perspectives into the conversation. But you're practicing a kind of listening that is penetrating. You're listening for the heart of what the other person has said, something the speaker may not even be able to hear himself. You are sifting through all the words and identifying core feelings, thoughts, beliefs or problems. In this case, you listened for the feeling that lies underneath your husband's work challenges. This is called *validating* an emotion, and it is powerful. When someone has had a feeling validated, it has a way of opening up the conversation. Things are about to get deep.

A third way to push the arrow toward the other person is by answering a question with a question. If I have learned anything as a listener over the past fifteen years, it's that people love to ask for advice, but when they ask for advice they don't usually want it; instead, they want an opportunity to discuss their struggle. Every generic request for advice has a personal story or trouble behind it. If you dispense advice too quickly, you are not hearing them. A simple response of "Why do you ask?" will take the conversation to the level of motivation, which is where the true meaning lies. Generally speaking, the more you can uncover what the other person truly wants to talk about, the better the conversation will go.

Finally, a way to keep the smart arrow hovering over the other person is through active listening. A passive listener offers little facial expression or responsiveness, staring blankly at the person speaking. Active listening acknowledges that a good conversation involves two engaged parties. In truth, the listener is probably working harder. To be an active listener is to visibly involve yourself in the interaction, helping the speaker to trust that you are present and engaged. The classic active listening expressions, in addition to good questions, are nods of the head, eye contact, sounds like "uh huh," "hmm" or "really?" and an attentive posture, like leaning forward and facing the speaker. I like to compare active listening to what I've experienced at some Pentecostal churches, where the congregation will nudge the preacher forward with vocal responses like "Amen" and "Go on, preacher!"[7] Active listening is a way of telling the speaker to go on. If you notice the speaker becoming more animated and alive in the conversation, you are practicing active listening. Keep going.

Active listening requires energy, which can be very difficult after a long day. Tiredness plays a significant factor in passive listening, which is a reason why I think it is most difficult to listen in our families. We are with our spouses and our children at our most tired moments of the day. It can be frustrating because we can spend all day listening to people that we may not be all that excited to listen to, and then when we are with the people we most want to listen to, we may lack the energy. Sometimes we need to be able to say, "I really want to hear this, but I am exhausted right now, and I can't give you my full attention. Can I listen to you in the morning?" I am of the opinion that short spells of active listening are far more valuable than long periods of half-hearted listening.

A way to gauge the skill of a listener is to gauge the quality of their responses. Listening does not mean remaining silent or staring blankly at the speaker. We can be certain that if a person is dispensing non sequiturs and conversational detours they are not listening well. A skilled listener will respond accurately and directly to what has been said, and her questions will flow organically from the conversation itself, not approach it as strangers.

TO UNDERSTAND BEFORE BEING UNDERSTOOD

O Divine Master, grant that I may not so much seek
To be consoled, as to console;
To be understood, as to understand;
To be loved as to love.[8]

The listening heart, taking its cue from the prayer of St. Francis, is one that seeks to understand before it is understood. This is a radical act in a self-justifying world, which is why we need to ask for strength from on high to pull it off. When I think about the patterns of my everyday conversations, I realize just how much effort I put toward clarifying and defending myself, trying to get the other person to understand *me*. Especially if there is a disagreement, I will expend massive amounts of energy trying to explain myself. What if I took that same energy and focused it on understanding the other person, seeking clarification when I am confused, gently asking questions that take us deeper into the other person's world?

A devoted listener knows that there is always more to learn about another person, no matter how long you've known them. There is always more to the story. There are more layers to unpack, more memories to relate, more fears to usher us into silence. It should not be lost on us that listening for understanding assumes we *don't* have understanding of the other person. How many con-flicts and disagreements start because we think we already·under-stand each other? Danger levels rise when we assume we know what the other person is going to say, what position they will take or what their *true* motives are.

We can actually start to respond to a person before they have even opened their mouth. That is one of the reasons why it's ac-tually harder to listen to people we have known for a long time, because we presume to already know them. We have lost the ability to be surprised by them. But good listening is always open to sur-prise. Listening takes seriously that other people are truly "other," that human beings are mysteries wrapped in flesh, infinitely sur-prising, and that no matter how long you've known a person you actually have little access to the deep things inside them. That is why sustained listening is required.

Listening for understanding and judging what we hear cannot coexist. If you are spending your energy evaluating and critiquing what the other person says, you do not have mental space to listen. A listener's job is not to stand outside of a situation and pronounce a verdict, declaring another person innocent or guilty, right or wrong. The kind of listening that I am advocating for is about entering into another person's world, getting our feet dirty in the layered soil of their lives. A judge aims to be impartial; a listener is decidedly partial. Listening for understanding means taking the side of the other person, trying to see and think and feel as they do, creatively imagining yourself into their world. You aim to understand their world from the inside. You can tell when you are offering someone a nonjudgmental listening presence because she will become increasingly open and vulnerable with you. If she starts closing down emotionally from you, she is likely feeling judged.

SLOW LISTENING

Ancient wisdom advises us to "be quick to listen, slow to speak." The second half of that sentence is not as catchy, but just as necessary: "slow to anger; for your anger does not produce God's righteousness" (James 1:19-20). James knows that more often than not our anger at others is about us, not them. There is such a thing as righteous anger, but it usually belongs to God; our version is usually contempt or arrogance. Our anger wants to change and control others, making them into people who have an uncanny resemblance to us. Listening offers the sacred gift of letting others be themselves. We let them have their own thoughts, feel their own feelings and believe their own beliefs without attacking them or running their words through our own critical filters. We aim to understand them on their terms, not ours.

Listening for understanding is slow. A good listener believes in taking the long route. That's why most of us don't do it. If I make a quick judgment and dispense some fast advice, then I can move on to the next thing. The truth is that your listening style reveals your lifestyle. If your life is saturated with busyness, hurry and distraction, then your listening will be scattered and rushed. Listening for understanding cannot be a mere checkbox on your to-do list. It requires your attention, concentration and observational skill.

This kind of listening always gets better over time, because the more often I listen to a person the more I learn about how they express themselves. In my work as a spiritual director, where I have the opportunity to listen to the same person on regular occasions, I have come to realize that listening for understanding is not only about understanding particular words a person says but understanding *how* they use words. Some people try to use as much logic and reasoning as possible; others use words as capsules of emotion. Some use humor to distract from their pain; others use hyperbole to draw attention to things of importance. A great listener becomes a student of each person's individual dialect.

Likewise, if I'm serious about listening for understanding I will listen to the nonverbal cues that constitute the vast majority of what a person is communicating. Listening experts say that only 7 percent of a person's meaning is conveyed in the actual words they speak. Fifty-five percent of communication is body language—gestures, eye contact, posture—and 38 percent is voice—tone, volume, speed and intensity in how you speak.[9] If we are going to use the phrase "body language" so regularly, then we should place equal emphasis on "body listening." A big part of this practice involves simply noticing. I notice when a person's eyes get red or light up, when they sit forward or slouch in their chair, when they trail off or look at the ground, how their voice gets louder or quivers. Most people intuitively know what these things mean, but we don't always pay attention to them or consider their meaning as we consider our response.

A GOOD EAR

If we want to understand before we are understood, we must deploy what John Steinbeck referred to as "a good ear."[10] A good ear is one that hears below the surface. Every text has a subtext, and it is usually the subliminal messages that have the most power and truth. It is a rule of human nature that we often say what we do not mean. We use words that are not true to how we feel. We distort and hide and obfuscate, usually because we fear presenting the real us and being rejected for it. Given this, if we want to be deep listeners we must listen between the lines to the silences, the emotions, the doubts, the deep-seated beliefs that influence a person's life, choices and self-image. We listen for the untold story.

There are often two simultaneous conversations happening

during one interaction. There is the word-level conversation, the conversation on display, and there is the conversation happening below the surface.

Here is a paraphrase of a conversation I had a few years ago with a student named Ryan, who was in his last semester of college. He had been having the same conversation about his future for weeks, and he was stuck on repeat. So I tried to listen to the wavelengths beneath the surface.

Ryan: I've been really wrestling with what to do after I graduate. I am deciding between missionary work and Teach for America. I have been thinking about it and praying about it and talking about it nonstop, but no answers are coming.

Adam: Why have you chosen those two options? What is their appeal for you?

Ryan: I don't know. I want to take what I have learned in college about God's heart for the world, and I want to apply it. I want my life to matter, and I want to help the poor.

Adam: Those are certainly good motivations. But thinking and talking and praying hasn't led to any clarity? Why do you think that is?

Ryan: I don't know! I have had probably one hundred conversations with people—my parents, my sister, my friends, my pastor—and nothing has seemed to help. I am even considering fasting and praying for several days.

Adam: That sounds pretty exhausting. You are trying really hard. I wonder if you're trying to control things too much.

Ryan: Why would I do that?

Adam: I don't know for sure. What do you think?

Ryan: I just want to do something worthwhile with my life. I don't want to get a job like everyone else and just make money. I guess I think that if I just get a job after college I'll settle into a routine and never do anything of real value.

Adam: Hmm. I wonder if you're feeling afraid. Often when we're acting controlling it's because we are afraid of something. What do you think?

Ryan: [After a long pause] I'm afraid of a lot of things. I'm afraid of graduating from college. I'm afraid of losing my faith after I graduate and settling into a lukewarm life. I'm afraid of being insignificant.

After that moment the conversation changed. We had identified a feeling—fear—underlying Ryan's dilemma. Feelings drive our behavior much more than rational thought. Once we had moved beyond his decision-making process to the emotions that were fueling it, we could make progress.

In this conversation we find a few themes that show up regularly when you listen for understanding. First, the presenting problem is not really what the conversation is about. If we had stayed with the pros and cons of missionary work or teaching, the conversation would have been a dead end.

Second, there is incredible power in naming emotions. You say the word, in the most basic way possible. *Afraid. Angry. Hurt. Ashamed. Sad.* Often you can see the physical reaction in the other person when you name their feeling. They let out a deep breath and relax, as though the unidentified feeling had been the pressure in their shoulders and the tightness in their neck.

Third, deep listening requires tentativeness. You don't know the answers, and you ask questions that you don't know the answers to.

It is not your role to sniff out motives like a detective in a whodunit mystery. This is because, and I can't stress this enough, *you are not the expert on another person's life.* They know themselves better than you ever will. The solution to their problems lies within them, and good listening involves helping another person find it, not solving their problems for them. You want to encourage the speaker to think for himself, so when you are listening well, you are practicing good guesswork. You ask careful questions, guess at emotions, clarify your confusion and do regular "check-ins" ("If I'm hearing you right, you are saying . . . Is that accurate?") to make sure you're on the right track.

THE LISTENER WHO SAVED THANKSGIVING

That awkward silence and the sound of chewing that you hear? That snarling two-headed monster of off-limit topics—religion and politics—has struck your Thanksgiving dinner table again. There are few other topics that cause mature adults to cover their ears and say, "Lalalalalalalalah!!!" It's no secret that, on the hot-button issues, everyone wants to filibuster and no one wants to listen. Even if we try to listen, most of us don't know how to listen in a way that builds empathy and brings us together. But I believe there is a way out of this holiday gridlock.

We need to start with the acknowledgment that our theological and political doctrines, as much as we want to think they are based on pure fact and logic, are deeply personal to us. Underneath our ideological platforms are emotional commitments, passionate beliefs about ourselves and the world, and personal experiences and relationships. When someone criticizes our politics or religion, they are not criticizing an issue; they are criticizing us and our bedrock beliefs about how the world works and how our lives hold together—or at least we think they are.

The good news for the listener is that there is a backstory to every theological story. People don't have dearly held beliefs because they read a book and found a good idea in it. There are stories inside of them, waiting to be told, and we can completely change the conversation if we can find those stories. One person believes in hell because he was abused as a child; another person doesn't believe in it because of her unbelieving but beloved grandmother. Often we believe something because someone we love believes it, and we show our gratitude and loyalty to that person by holding their belief.

If we want to cut through the rhetoric and circular debate, we can explore why other people hold their beliefs. We're not trying to sniff out motives like a dog at the airport or falling victim to the genetic fallacy—the logical error that assumes if I have pinpointed the source of a person's belief then I have therefore disproved that belief. We are motivated by curiosity and empathy. And our best friend is the "why" question. Instead of giving a counterargument to someone's point, the listener asks why a person believes that.

Here are a few good why questions that can be used in a variety of theological and personal conversations. When someone is passionate about something, there is almost always a personal reason behind it.

- Why do you hold that belief?
- Why is that important to you?
- Why does that bother you?
- Why did that hurt you?
- Why do you feel that way?

Here are a few more that don't start with why but get at the same idea:

- When did you start believing that?
- This seems very personal for you—is there a reason for that?
- What role has God played in helping you form that belief?

CONVERSATIO DIVINA

As we near the end of this chapter, I want to say clearly what I have hinted at all along: our standards for conversations are too low. Too often we treat them as a social transaction, an exchange of ideas, an information dump. What we expect out of conversations is routinely what we will get out of them.

The practice of a conversation is a sacred art. Meaningful conversations are essential parts of God's ongoing rescue of us. This is why we can expect that every now and then, in the midst of an ordinary conversation, a Presence that transcends the physical space of the room will visit. And a Word that exceeds the cumulative wisdom of the people in conversation may whisper.

What if we came to understand the most important conversations as prayer? When people resolve to probe beneath the surface of everyday life, to walk through the halls of small talk into the threshold of mystery, we can be assured that our conversation happens in communion with the Spirit. My seminary professor Deborah Van Deusen Hunsinger writes that "there is a divine drama hidden in all of us, crying out to be heard."[11] Sacred conversation seeks to listen for that divine drama, that redemptive story, the tale of lost and found again that is written on our souls. With this perspective, a conversation does not have one speaker and one listener but always two listeners. When two or more listen in his name, Jesus listens too. It's not a bad idea to leave a chair empty to remind us.

We could modify the practice of *lectio divina* slightly to create a *conversatio divina*, the practice of sacred conversation. The foundation of *conversatio* is the belief that God is present in and guides the conversations we give him as offerings, and some that we don't. We listen not only to another person but to the voice that speaks in, through and in spite of human voices. Then we are free to let go of tight agendas and the need to steer the conversation where we think it should go. We open ourselves to letting it go gently off course and to taking surprising directions and divine detours.

A challenge I face when listening to someone on this level is feeling flooded by the wall of words that come my way. If I try to absorb every word or treat each one with the same weight, I get lost and confused. I have learned that my goal is not to try to memorize their message so I can repeat back every word. The best kind of listening is not one that receives information like a satellite dish; the best kind of listening is one that pierces, pushing toward the deepest, most basic truths. Sacred listening requires discernment over what to hold on to and what to let slip by. Just as I listen for God's specific word spoken to me amid all the words in a text, I listen in a conversation for the words or phrases that carry particular weight with them. Not every word and theme requires the same attention. Sometimes a person digresses or spends time on a topic that seems less central to the conversation, and we let those ideas drift by. Other times a person casually waves at an idea or feeling that strikes us as deeply important.

In *conversatio divina* we listen for repeated words or themes. If a person continually circles back to a question or a relationship or an idea, we know it deserves our attention. We pay attention to words that carry deep feelings, along with the accompanying body language and facial expressions that bear those feelings. Some of the most revealing moments are when a word hangs in the air, echoing through the listeners, lingering even after they have moved on in the conversation. We listen for those authentic moments, those truly human moments when someone reveals herself to us, when the mask, even just for a second, comes off and we meet the real person.

The impact of a moment in a conversation is often more powerful than the words spoken. Trust your instincts. The other person's heart is speaking to you, and God may be speaking to you through it. If you feel confused by what they are saying, trust your confusion. Ask them to slow down or to approach from a simpler angle. Your confusion probably echoes their own tangled thoughts, and it may indicate that they are avoiding the heart of the matter. Listen to the voice of the Spirit while you listen to the other person. Don't listen for what truth or insight you should speak to them. Listen for what questions to ask.

Ryan, who earlier was wrestling over which direction to take after college, didn't end up in either Teach for America or missionary work upon graduation. When I asked him the question "Are you afraid?" it helped him to see his dilemma in a new way and to realize that the career decision was actually incidental to the heart of his struggle. He decided not to let his fear push him into something he wasn't ready for. What continually amazes me about listening interactions is that a person can walk away without any new insight into the problem they brought with them, and yet see things so differently. That day Ryan and I made no progress in determining his career, yet he came away with clarity and peace. A place of peace and rest is where the best decisions are made. Listening helps us get there.

SEVEN

Listening to People in Pain

FEW THINGS SHUT DOWN A PERSON in pain faster than quoting the Bible at them. As I write that, I can hear the sirens of the Heresy Police surrounding my building. Yes, the Bible contains the words of life, the promises of God with us that have comforted saints and resurrected sinners. But the Bible can also be the ultimate conversation killer. It can be used as a tool for silencing people and for short-circuiting grief, hurt and depression. Sometimes people use the Bible in a way that makes hurting people feel like God is telling them to shut up.

This chapter is based on two premises. First, life is hard. If you haven't experienced that yet, just wait a little while longer. If you are in a sunny season of life, by all means bask in it, because a storm front is not far away. Second, many of us are at a loss for how to respond to a person who is experiencing that life is hard. We are daunted by the weight and emotion of painful situations, and our best intentions seem inadequate. We say too much or we say too little, we quote the wrong verse or feel a compulsive need to quote a verse at all, we do the wrong thing or we do the right thing wrongly, or whatever we say or do falls with a thud.

I don't like saying this, but it has been my experience that Christians are often worse at dealing with people in pain than others with different beliefs. Truth be told, I have chosen on many occasions to share my painful moments and emotions with non-Christians rather than Christians because I knew I would be better heard. Dietrich Bonhoeffer lamented the same thing: "Many people are looking for an ear that will listen. They do not find it among Christians, because these Christians are talking when they should be listening."[1] This saddens me and confuses me. It seems to me that Christians should run into the fire like no one else, because we follow a Savior who descended into hell. No one should be better equipped to respond to suffering than those who wear crosses around their neck. But it is far less messy to stand over people in pain than it is to enter their worlds and risk feeling pain ourselves.

I once heard a ministry colleague say, "I'm going to be with a person in the hospital tonight. Time to speak some truth." This idea prevails in many Christian circles, that *preaching* is the healing balm for suffering. Whether it's sickness or divorce or job loss, a crisis calls for some sound biblical exhortation. I have a number of issues with this. First, it assumes that hurting people do not believe the right things or believe with enough fervency. They may end up receiving the message that their faith is not strong enough for them to see their situation rightly, or that something is wrong with them because they are struggling. Second, preaching to people in pain preys on the vulnerable. It's stabbing the sword of truth into their wound or doing surgery without anesthesia. Unwelcome truth is never healing. Third, "speaking truth" into situations of pain is distancing. You get to stand behind your pulpit or your intercessory prayer that sounds a lot like a sermon, and the other person is a captive audience, trapped in the pew of your anxious truth. Suffering inevitably makes a person feel small and isolated, and preaching to them only makes them feel smaller and more alone, like a scolded child.

Dr. Seuss wrote some classic stories, but he also gave some classically bad advice: "Don't cry that it's over. Smile that it happened."[2] Your role as a listener is, by all means, to let them cry that it's over. Don't be the Grinch who stole grief. Be a witness to their tears. Each falling tear carries pain, and it's the only way to get it out.

A hurting person is in a storm. They are cold, wet, shivering and scared. Preaching, platitudes and advice will not get them out of the storm. Don't tell someone in a storm that it's a sunny day. There will likely come a day when the clouds part, but it is not today. It's not your job to pull them out of the storm. It's your job to get soaked with them.

ENTERING IN

The listener's job is to enter in. The apostle Paul nails it with these verses:

> Blessed be the God and Father of our Lord Jesus Christ, the Father of mercies and the God of all consolation, who consoles us in all our affliction, so that we may be able to console those who are in any affliction with the consolation with which we ourselves are consoled by God. For just as the sufferings of Christ are abundant for us, so also our consolation is abundant through Christ. If we are being afflicted, it is for your consolation and salvation; if we are being consoled, it is for your consolation, which you experience when you patiently endure the same sufferings that we are also suffering. Our hope for you is unshaken; for we know that as you share in our sufferings, so also you share in our consolation. (2 Corinthians 1:3-7)

There is no getting around the fact that a Christian community is one that suffers. The pioneer of our faith suffered, the main symbol of our tradition is one of agony and death, and it's no use trying to remove the cruciform marks from the hands and feet of the church. The mark of the gospel is not health and wealth, but nails and blood. The good news is that a Christian community is one that suffers *together*. We partake in one another's sufferings, an unsavory meal that is made sweeter when we patiently endure with one another. Consolation is not necessarily rescue from suffering but what comes as we suffer together. This does not at all mean that the church ignores injustice, poverty and oppression, or that we do not seek to relieve suffering when we have the ability to do so. We rail against pain and rage at death, because we know things are not as they ought to be. But there are many times in life when we just don't have the ability to relieve someone's suffering, as much as we wish we did. You're not going to magically remove someone's grief when a loved one dies or snap away their depression when a dream fails. The grief and depression are essential parts of that person's healing. The church is a community of people who acknowledge suffering, treat it as real and enter into one another's pain, because our Lord knows our afflictions. Jesus offers his presence in suffering, and so should we.

We are eager to offer up premature consolation though, aren't we? I call it *preemptive assurance*. If we can strike first with our assurances and answer some questions that haven't been asked, maybe we can protect ourselves from discomfort. We start hearing ourselves say things like:

- "Everything will be okay."
- "Hang in there."
- "God is good."

- "This will pass."
- "Soon you will be glad this happened."
- "God is in control."
- "This will make you stronger."
- "God won't test you beyond what you are able to handle."
- "God works all things for good."

When my language takes on a particularly religious slant, I am probably dispensing some preemptive assurance. Pain is too serious for pat answers and glib God-talk. When I was starting out as a chaplain, I had an itchy prayer trigger finger. My first question for a patient was "How are you feeling?" and my second question was "Can I pray for you?" That way I could maintain control and let my carefully rehearsed prayers drown out their pain. I would move on to the next hospital room thinking I had done my job. I hadn't.

Listening to people in pain is about giving them room to grieve and weep and rage and doubt. We're not there to spiritualize their pain or theologize their experience. Our religious talk, preemptive assurance and breezy conversation take space, when instead we want to give space. Otherwise we are subject to Job's rebuke: "I have heard many such things; miserable comforters are you all. Have windy words no limit? Or what provokes you that you keep on talking?" (Job 16:2-3). Bonhoeffer said it almost as strongly: "It must be a decisive rule of every Christian fellowship that each individual is prohibited from saying much that occurs to him."[3] In other words, listening and silence are not necessarily the same thing, but silence is a really good start. Some situations are so heavy that only silence can support their weight.

We are on the wrong track when we diminish the emotions that people are feeling. You don't tell them how to feel; you let them feel however they are feeling, in the presence of another. Don't catch what I call "at-least syndrome." At least you have your health. At least you got to have her in your life for a little while. At least it's not as bad as what this other person is experiencing. "At least" statements diminish pain. Let people have their pain. In some situations, it's all they have.

It's a scary prospect, especially if you are uncomfortable with raw emotion, but you need to let people feel their hurt. This is especially challenging when you have done something to hurt someone. You might find yourself whipping out the "quick on the draw" apology. The faster I can apologize, the less I have to listen to their pain and the less guilty I can feel! The quick apology is not for them but for you. If you can't hear the pain that you played a role in inflicting, there will not be full reconciliation.

Sometimes we not only encourage people to express their pain but even help them to feel what they are feeling more intensely. As a hospice chaplain, I was surprised to discover that my role was often not to reassure but to remind people just how agonizing their situation was. They would take a step toward describing their pain, then take a step back and offer a cliché like "But that's the circle of life for you." That's when I would step in and say, "Yeah, but the circle of life sucks, doesn't it?" Sometimes you have to say the blunt thing to open the floodgates. Too much tiptoeing and nothing significant ever gets uncovered. I gave them permission to grieve and to express their pain in the simplest, rawest way possible, which is the language of deep emotion.

THE MORTAL ENEMY OF LISTENING: ANXIETY

Neurological research has discovered that when a person near us expresses sadness, our bodies involuntarily respond to them. Our brains contain "mirror neurons," which automatically mimic what we see in the facial expressions and body language of another person. If a person wears a frown, then our mouths, on a micro-level, will start to frown without any conscious decision on our part, and those undetectable movements will actually produce similar feelings in us.[4] If someone is sad, our mouths curl downward, our tear ducts are activated, and we start to feel sad. The primal compassionate response is built into us. Our bodies want to feel the pain of others.

It's when we voluntarily open those mouths that have involuntarily responded with compassion that we screw things up. Our bodies may want to feel their pain but the rest of us doesn't. It is an axiom of human nature that we avoid pain, and to that end, we avoid other people who are in pain. If we can't physically avoid them, we emotionally avoid them. We try to fix, solve, rescue, give advice or make the pain go away, which usually makes things worse.

Anxiety is the mortal enemy of listening to people in pain. When people are struggling with pain, sickness, loss, doubt, inner conflict or broken relationships it inevitably stirs up our own anxiety. We hear our lives and vulnerability in theirs. The closer we are to a person, and the more our lives are interwoven with theirs, the lower our anxiety threshold. When they question the direction of their life, they question the direction of *our* life. When they hurt, it disrupts our sense of well-being too.[5]

We have the hardest time listening when things become personal for us. When something upsets us, whether in a close relationship or in a situation we are more removed from, it is usually because it hits close to home in some way. The reason we have a hard time hearing the doubts and faith questions of others is that it provokes our own unacknowledged doubts. We have a hard time holding together the tension of our God's goodness and our world's brokenness, and our anxiety makes us rush to simplistic answers.

We are unable to sit in mystery with others because it brings us face to face with our own pain, our own questions, our own faith struggles.

For six months I volunteered as a counselor at a food bank affiliated with my church. Clients would come in a few nights a week and talk with us before going home with their donated food and clothes. We were in the throes of the worst recession of most of our lifetimes. Our client logs were at a record high. Their stories were heartbreaking. One man was a homeless Vietnam vet. An older woman was taking care of her disabled son and living on food stamps. A young mother came in with her two young daughters the Tuesday before Thanksgiving.

I myself was unemployed, laid off six months before I started volunteering. I had applied for dozens of jobs, in several different industries, but the competition in a recession was stiff. Low-paying jobs would have one hundred applicants. I started volunteering at the food bank partly because I needed something to do. The circumstances of the clients I saw every week were much bleaker than mine, but I couldn't help but see myself in their situations. Our conversations provoked some of my deepest fears about the future and my deepest doubts about God. I would go home and lie on the couch in a fetal position. And truth be told, even with all my training, I practiced some of my worst listening with our clients. I know that when I start doing things quickly, my anxiety is speaking for me. I would end conversations quickly, pray quickly and refer people to other agencies quickly. Good listening is slow; anxiety moves fast.

ANXIETY AND THE LIMINAL

When we listen to someone in pain we enter into a liminal place. The liminal place is the in-between, the tightrope walk between two cliffs, suspended in midair. Pain has taken them out of their previously comfortable place, but they have not yet reached a new resting point. They can't turn back. We don't know how long this harrowing journey will take, nor where it will lead them. We can't see the other side. That is why the most authentic conversations are the ones that can go unresolved. Conversations with people in pain rarely wrap up like an episode of *Scooby-Doo*. People don't walk away fixed, their hearts fully mended, their mysteries neatly tied up.

If I want to be a comfort to a person in pain, I must be able to wander in the liminal place with them. I will take their pain, and the tension that it creates, seriously. I will take this moment that you are currently in—with all its meaning, uncertainty, doubt and pain—seriously, because you are loved, right now. Everything that you bring to the table, without filter or editing or resolution, has significance. Listening is not a reward for good behavior or proper doctrine. I am not waiting for you to be fixed, say things perfectly, believe what I do or see things as I do before I listen to you. If Jesus had listened like that, he would have spent a lot of time alone.

It is the Light that enables us to be there with them in their darkness. This kind of listening embraces mystery and ambiguity and, perhaps hardest of all, waiting. It is able to sit with the questions without grasping immediately for answers. It admits that I don't know the outcome and it is not my job to steer the conversation where I want it to go.

But the liminal place is an anxious place. Many of us have a low threshold for the unresolved. We are eager to turn to the last page and read from there, but that doesn't honor the unfinished story of the other person. When we try to help someone in pain, we often end up saying or doing things, subconsciously, to assuage our own anxiety. Let's be honest: we often want others to be okay so we can feel okay. We want them to feel better and move on so our lives can return to normal. We try to control the conversation as a way of compensating for our anxiety.

Our approach to people in pain can amount to self-therapy. We start to feel that tightening in our chest, that knot of anxiety in our stomachs, and we want our heart to stop accelerating. So we take another's situation as an opportunity to soothe and reassure ourselves, but we miss them in the process because we are too busy projecting onto them. So, a good question to ask yourself before you venture to speak into such situations is *Who am I trying to reassure here?* Am I trying to convince someone else that this situation isn't so bad, or am I trying to convince *myself* that this situation isn't so bad? Am I trying to rush them to the other side so that *my* life will feel more stable?

THE LISTENER'S JOB: EMPATHY

What pain calls for is empathy. *Empathy* literally means "to feel into"; when we act with empathy we seek to enter, as much as possible, into the world of another person. This is an imaginative process, as we temporarily put on their clothes and live their lives, think their thoughts, hear with their ears and feel their feelings. We are trying to understand their situation, insofar as it is possible, from the inside out. We don't break down a person's thoughts into what we agree with or disagree with, approve of or disapprove of, because we are trying to *be* them for a short time. We are, in the words of William Ury, "stepping to the side" of the other person.[6]

I am convinced that a listener who knows how to empathize can talk with anyone about anything. Sometimes we shy away from people in pain because we have not personally suffered what they are going through. My parents are alive, so I can't help my friend who just lost his father. I am healthy, so I should let someone else who has survived cancer care for my coworker who was just diagnosed. But empathy does not require me to have undergone identical experiences as another person. In fact, if I have experienced the same thing I may be tempted to turn the conversation toward myself or project onto the other person my memories, pain or solutions. Of course, sometimes it is helpful to experientially know the pain of another's experience, but live long enough and everyone will relate to grief, loss, bereavement, shame and broken relationships. Empathy chooses to enter into the dark places of another's world, to shiver in the cold with them, and to wait with them.

KILLING THE MOMENT

There is a running joke between my parents that when someone expresses excitement and the other person responds with something less than excitement, the first person says, "Well, you killed that moment." For example:

Mom: "I just had my annual review at the hospital and they really love the work I'm doing!"

Dad: "Does this mean you're going to be working more days?"

Mom: "Well, you killed that moment."

We kill the moment when we are unable, or unwilling, to identify the tone in the other person's words and to match it in ours. If we want to save the moment, we could employ the same strategy we use when reading a biblical text. To rightly read the book of Revelation, for example, we must place it in the literary genre of apocalypse, which uses veiled symbolism and otherworldly imagery to describe historical events and people. If we want to listen empathically to another person, we must identify the "genre" of their speech patterns, namely the emotional content of what they say and how they say it.

Listening for genre is another way of saying, "Rejoice with those who rejoice, weep with those who weep" (Romans 12:15). Joy calls for joy, humor calls for laughter, and sadness calls for sadness. If someone is hurting, you will not help them by responding with detached, logical questions. If someone speaks loudly and animatedly, a quiet, subdued tone will feel deflating, even controlling. Some people mirror others instinctively, but some struggle with an emotional tone deafness, which prevents them from hearing cues in speech patterns and responding appropriately. The good news is that it can be learned. Listening to genre does not mean acting or faking it, but it does require you to access those parts of yourself that know the emotions and experiences of the other person. If you have not explored the grieving part of yourself, you will likely be ineffective at listening to the grief of others.

If you take the pain, doubts and struggles of another person seriously, then hopefully they will start to take them seriously for themselves. Those of us in certain Christian circles have been so conditioned to sweep away faith questions and doubts with religious platitudes that we don't even know how to embrace the process that our pain initiates. We say that God uses all things for good, but we don't know how to participate in that process of redemption because we can't acknowledge that we are in pain, that our beliefs are shaken and that the way we think, feel and live is changed. We are unable to get to the good that God works because we cannot face the bad that life brings. If some of us can lead by listening to people in pain, then perhaps we can start to change the culture that veils and minimizes pain. If we don't chide others for their faith struggles then maybe they will stop chiding themselves as well.

WEEPING AND HEALING

When Lazarus died, Jesus raised him, but the first thing he did was weep. He raised his cry with the grief of the community, the mourners exclaiming, "See how he loved him!" Jesus showed his love for Lazarus by weeping. And then he walked into the tomb and healed him. He entered the pain and then entered the tomb. We fail people in pain when we try to heal them before weeping.

Pain, whether physical, emotional or spiritual, is so unsettling because it reminds us that we are finite. It confronts us with death. Sometimes sick people sign a DNR—"Do not resuscitate," a legal document that guarantees that paramedics will not take "heroic measures" (CPR or life support) in order to save them if they go into cardiac arrest or stop breathing. I wonder if we should all view people in significant pain as having signed emotional DNRs. We are not trying to protect them from pain or even the type of death that results from lost dreams, lost relationships or a lost sense of invincibility. We are not trying to rush them from Palm Sunday to Easter, bypassing Good Friday. Things often need to get worse before they get better, and so we do not stand above the pit, detached, trying to throw them the rope of advice or impassioned defenses of God's goodness. We go down into the pit with them, weeping with them, letting our heart break with the heartbroken, waiting together for resurrection.

A few years ago a student leader I worked with, Karri, had this conversation with another student, Sarah.

Sarah: "I'm worthless."

Karri: "No, you're not."

Sarah: "No one loves me."

Karri: "Yes, they do."

Sarah: "God hates me."

Karri: "No, he doesn't. He loves you."

Sarah: "I can't do anything right. I'm a failure."

Karri: "No, you're not. Look at all you've accomplished!"

So much of that conversation rings true. A role of fellow believers is to remind us of who we are, to advocate for us when we are weak, to represent God to us when he seems far away. We are aghast when someone we love feels worthless, and we rush to them like white blood cells to an invading virus. Everything that Karri said in that conversation with Sarah was true. But here's the problem. Karri stood outside the pit that held Sarah, looking in, trying to argue Sarah out of her feelings.

It is common for people to speak declaratively and factually when they are truly telling us how they feel. What Sarah meant was "I *feel* like God hates me" and "I *feel* like a failure." Unbeknownst to Karri, her reactions, as well intentioned as they were, dismissed Sarah's feelings. Sarah was in the pit, and Karri stood at the opening above and tried to drag her out. It's as effective as trying to coax buds into blossoming in January. Instead, Karri needed to go down into the pit. This would have been better:

Sarah: "I'm worthless."

Karri: "I'm so sorry to hear that you feel that way. That must be so painful."

Sarah: "God hates me."

Karri: "Wow. That's an awful feeling to have."

Sarah: "I'm a failure. I can't do anything right."

Karri: "That's such a heavy burden to carry."

Instead of "speaking truth," in this instance Karri is empathizing with Sarah, going down into the pit of despair with her. And now together, as two fragile and flawed human beings, they wait for resurrection, the work that only God can do.

In order to do this, Karri must put on Sarah's emotional world, and she may have to access similar feelings and experiences she herself has had. The part of this that is so difficult and confusing for many people is that you actually encourage the other person to *stay in the feeling*. It is not your job to rescue them or even to try and make them feel better. It almost feels like you are digging the pit deeper rather than trying to pull them out. You have to even be careful about questions in these situations, because some questions can inadvertently take the other person out of their heart and into their head. If, in the moment of hurt, you ask something like "Have you ever felt this way before?" you can almost see their energy go from their bodies to their brains, out of the feeling and into their thoughts. Then you are no longer addressing the heart of the matter.

I can practically hear the objections of readers yelling at this book. Do we just leave people in despair? Do we wallow with them in their feelings and offer no way out? Do we all perish in the pit? My first response is, you would be surprised what can happen through empathic listening. Instead of only telling someone that God loves them, you show them that God loves them through bearing their pain with them.

The most critical element in speaking truth is not content or conviction but timing. People in pain are unlikely to hear unless they have first felt heard. The most biblical sermon, preached at the wrong time, will fall as flat as a wedding sermon preached at a funeral. People will be defensive, or silent, if the sword of truth is wielded at the wrong time. Don't confuse their silence for agreement. But if they feel listened to and loved, then they may be able to hear the promises of God on the other side. Then they may be receptive to a question like "What do you need right now?"[7] They may able to start thinking about the future and what new life God may be offering them.

Listeners weep and then heal.

EIGHT

Listening to Your Life

I HAVE A LOT OF VOICES IN MY HEAD. I relate to the man Jesus encounters who is possessed by a spirit called Legion, so named because "we are many." Tossed to and fro by the spirits who control him, uncertain which way is up and which way is down, he is confused, scared and isolated. To a lesser degree, I get that. I have days when my mind seems filled with a legion of voices, a thousand instructors, warriors and accusers who do not agree with one another and do not like each other. Some of them are louder than others. Some of them are seductive. Some sound a lot like my parents. Some of them are jerks. Some of them throw two-year-old temper tantrums. Some whisper, some shout. Sometimes they are amusing. Other times they leave me feeling confused and divided. They are many, that is certain, and sometimes I wish they would all charge over the cliff into the sea.

Now before you think my doctor should up my meds or strap me into a bed, know that there are others who hear the voices too. Walt Whitman famously said, "Do I contradict myself? Very well then I contradict myself, I am large, I contain multitudes." My spiritual director likens the voices in his head to a classroom of seventh graders. You have one kid looking out the window, you have one raising her hand to answer every question, one thinking about sex, one who is counting down to lunch, one who cheats on tests, one who is acting out for attention and another who bullies all the rest of them. You are their teacher trying desperately to supervise them and get them focused on the same task. Sometimes you tantalize them with rewards for good behavior, sometimes you have to send one of them to the principal's office, sometimes you bring one up to write on the board, and sometimes you just need them to all put their heads down on their desks and be quiet for a while.

It is the presence of the voices that has prompted many searching discussions in our spiritual tradition about *discernment*. Discernment involves paying attention to the interior movements of the soul—our thoughts, feelings, impulses, motivations, stirrings and everything else that happens within us. Many teachers have framed these conversations in terms of 1 John 4:1: "Beloved, do not believe every spirit, but test the spirits to see whether they are from God." From that text, Ignatius of Loyola developed his spirituality of the "discernment of spirits." Discernment is a testing, a sifting through of internal experiences—not only the purely "spiritual" but also the emotional, rational and physical—for the sake of embracing the good and turning your back on the bad. It involves the radical notion that if we want to hear God's voice, then perhaps we don't need to ascend to the heights of heaven into ethereal and abstract realms. Maybe we can start by listening to our lives.[1]

Discerning the voices starts with this foundation: *what takes place in you matters and has meaning.* It seems basic, but some will resist. Often I hear Christians say that the path to spiritual maturity involves "forgetting myself" and directing all my attention toward God, making little of me and much of him. While we aim to glorify God in all we do, the way of following Jesus is not self-abdication. Yes, we set aside what is passing away—the old ways, the old life, the old self—and then we become fully alive by taking on our new creation life, our truest and deepest self. We do not forget ourselves; we become fully ourselves. As St. Irenaeus in the second century said, "The glory of God is a human fully alive." We are not fully alive until we love God with all our mind, heart, soul and strength, and we cannot love God with all of ourselves unless we are well acquainted with our minds, hearts, souls and bodies. I believe that Christians should be leading the way in self-knowledge because, as John Calvin instructs us in his *Institutes*, "without knowledge of self there is no knowledge of God."

Your thoughts, emotions, impulses, desires, values, passions, dreams, recurring questions and bodily responses have meaning, are trying to teach you, and are all interconnected. They are telling you what your life is like. The voices that you choose to listen to are shaping what kind of person you are becoming. You can try to ignore them or avoid them, but if you do, you will be acting out of them unawares, sleepwalking to the step of your unconscious internal world. The realities that operate beneath the surface always hold the most sway. Instead, let's wake up to what is taking place inside of us, to listen to it, honor it and let it shape us into who we wish to be. As Parker Palmer has said so well, "Before I can tell my life what I want to do with it, I must listen to my life telling me who I am."[2] If we are going to take the doctrine of the indwelling Holy Spirit seriously, we must be open to the idea that God is speaking *within* us, not only from places and words *outside* of us. Deep things are stirring inside of us. Will we listen?

Discernment is the opposite of what most of us are inclined to do with the internal voices, especially the negative ones. They are so much easier to ignore, silence, push away, anesthetize or choke with food and drink. In cynical moments, I think we have constructed whole worlds to prevent us from listening to what is happening inside of us. Our cultural options for evading the voices are endless. The technology in our pockets guarantees that we never need have a quiet moment by ourselves. The circular debates, controversies and conflicts on the Internet promise that we can always find an outlet for our angst. We are buried in avalanches of distraction, escapism, entertainment, hyperactivity and addiction. Overwork, overscheduling and over-everything keep our lives full and our souls lonely. And we all know it is much more appetizing to stuff our feelings down with food rather than try to digest painful emotions.

The pace and activity of modern life are not all-consuming forces that we have no control over, uproariously sweeping into our lives like Vikings into a peaceful seafront village. We are usually glad for the distraction, because we are terrified of what will come if we sit in the quiet. Richard Rohr notes that the first things that show up after Jesus is driven into the wilderness are the wild beasts.[3] There are bright, menacing eyes in the dark. We might discover that we have deeply buried pain, anger, ungrieved losses, fears and hidden sins, not to mention unfulfilled dreams and desires. So we run as far and as fast as we can. Jesus went into the wilderness to face the voices, but we flee out of the wilderness, away from the voices and into the warm glow of distraction.

But isn't listening to yourself, so the objection might go, an exercise in self-absorption, an excuse for narcissistic navel gazing? Isn't focusing on myself the very definition of pride? Aren't we supposed to be people of love who lose ourselves in the service of others? I believe that good listening starts at home. How you listen to yourself will determine how you listen to others. Do you dismiss your own emotions? Then there is a good chance you will make a regular habit of dismissing the emotions of others. Those who are able to discern their own emotions will be most responsive to the emotions of others. If you are not able to sit with your own painful emotions, you will likely dispense dismissive advice and religious clichés to others when they are in pain. Do you quickly judge and condemn the thoughts and stirrings of your inner world? Then you will be unable to show compassion to others when they risk sharing with you. The harsher your own internal voices, the harsher will be your responses to the mistakes and shortcomings of others. You will be likely to project your own insecurities and anxieties onto others.

Self-discovery is not the ultimate end of listening to your life; love is. If we want to listen to others with compassion, gentleness and attentiveness, then we must learn to listen to ourselves with those same qualities. If we do the work in the quiet spaces, our compulsions will come out less when it's loud.

A FORCED QUIET: IGNATIUS OF LOYOLA

There are times when our lives come to resemble a vigorously shaken snow globe. There may be an idyllic cottage in there, a happy wisp of smoke curling out of the chimney, but we can't see it for the raging blizzard. As Madeleine L'Engle puts it, "When I am constantly running there is no time for being. When there is no time for being there is no time for listening."[4] Listening requires *being*. And when the wind is blowing and the snow is swirling, it is hard to be. That is when we need to stoke the fire, take a few deep breaths, let the snow settle and sit in the quiet.

Ignatius of Loyola, the sixteenth-century Spaniard who founded the order of the Jesuits and is now the patron saint of all spiritual retreats,[5] is known for many spiritual developments, but none more important than his nuanced teachings on discernment and paying attention to the affective movements of the soul. It is not a coincidence that he came upon his spiritual revelations in a forced season of quiet and seclusion.

Struck by a cannonball in the Italian War, Ignatius spent months in convalescence, passing the solitary hours reading and dreaming. His daily readings alternated between stories of knightly deeds and spiritual texts about the life of Jesus and monastics such as Francis of Assisi. Slowly, in his forced solitude he began to pay attention to what was taking place emotionally in himself as he read and reflected on different books. He swooned over the biographies of larger-than-life men and their lusty adventures, but after he closed the book his internal world took a turn toward the melancholy, saddened by the relative emptiness and fading glory of earthly conquests. His heart also exulted as he read about Jesus and St. Francis, but after he closed the book he found his heart still satisfied and inspired. Ignatius started to become aware of the Holy Spirit's work in his life when he experienced lasting joy, love, peace and contentment—what he called "consolations"—and he detected the movements of other powers when he experienced lasting emptiness, despair, lack of faith and spiritual depression, or "desolations."

Ignatius learned what anyone who experiments with solitude learns: the quiet gets loud real quick. In the outer silence the inner volume is turned up, and we must finally face the voices that speak. Silence doesn't muffle the voices; it amplifies them. And the quiet can be terrifying, lonely, desolate, the inner world's ghost town. Dallas Willard suggested that we hate the quiet because its inactivity and emptiness evokes death. Avoiding quiet might be the internal equivalent of the modern practice of building cemeteries out of public view.

Intentionally seeking the quiet requires courage. It is the courage to listen to yourself without the noise and distraction of others, without the validation of colleagues and family, without the glow of professional and personal accomplishments, and to sit in the stark, fragile reality of you. You give space for your behaviors, emotions, memories and body to speak to you. It requires not simply quiet but honest quiet; you must listen to what is really true about you—both the good and the bad, the heaven and the hell in each one of us. I am inspired by Marian Wright Edelman's line: "Learn to be quiet enough to hear the genuine within yourself so that you can hear it in others."[6]

LOVING YOUR ENEMY VOICES

Quiet and solitude are the training ground for listening to ourselves. Our everyday lives can become so saturated with busyness and hurry that we find ourselves spinning like the Tasmanian devil. By consciously removing ourselves from that pace for short periods of dedicated listening, we can train ourselves to listen and live slowly in all spheres of life. We can sit for ten or fifteen minutes and invite the voices to speak and to teach us.

The key to listening to your life is to take in what you hear without immediately appraising, judging or condemning it. You are giving the voices permission to speak, and you are listening to notice, not attack or silence them. You sit with them as though you are sitting in your living room listening to a friend.[7] Some of the whispers—the kind ones, the loving ones, the confident ones—are easier to befriend than the ones that growl—the self-doubting voices, the tempting voices, the accusing voices. But I believe they all have something to teach us. Loving your enemies will also mean learning to love the enemy voices in your head. What if we approached the harsh voices not with disdain but with empathy? What if we treated them with gentleness just as we would a hurting friend? The negative voices speak the way they do because they have wounds. If we seek to understand them, to know where they come from and why they say what they do, and even to laugh with them, we will find that they lose some of their power over us. Laboring to silence the voices seems far less effective than listening to them and asking them gentle questions. As Father Rohr puts it, "In terms of soul work, we dare not get rid of the pain before we have learned what it has to teach us."[8]

THE DISCERNMENT OF VOICES

What Ignatius of Loyola called "spirits," by which he meant the internal and affective movements of the soul, I am calling "voices."[9] When I say "the discernment of voices" I mean this: *listening to the internal voices and naming them.* Naming the voices is critical because it helps us understand them and also gives us some control over them. William Ury notes that "in ancient mythology, calling an evil spirit by its name enabled you to ward it off."[10] Identifying and naming the voices helps us break the spell they have over us. Calling out the voices helps us move from blindly reacting to them to consciously addressing them.

It is a helpful exercise to try to name the voices that speak in our heads. If the idea of naming the voices inside your head makes you feel like a crazy person, well, know that simply doing what the voices tell you to do may make you more crazy. Here are some of the negative internal voices I have named:

The parent: This is the voice telling me what I *should* be doing, what I'm doing wrong and that I'm not eating enough vegetables.

The therapist: He psychoanalyzes and diagnoses everyone around me, conveniently keeping a comfortable distance from real intimacy and having to look at myself.

The defendant: Everything that happens to me is someone else's fault. I was minding my own business, and other people are hurting me for no reason.

The critic: He watches people like he's watching a movie, and he nitpicks and finds something wrong with everyone, especially when they make mistakes that resemble my mistakes.

The lawyer: This is the voice that crafts brilliant defense arguments for my actions, even when no one is accusing me of anything.

The doomsayer: Everything that can go wrong, will go wrong. I will lose my job, all my friends will turn their backs on me, and I will die in a storm drain.

The balcony guys: These are like the guys from *The Muppet Show* who sit up in a balcony and sarcastically make fun of everybody.

The junior higher: This guy is ridiculously insecure and self-conscious. He is also a little narcissist. He always thinks people are staring at him.

The bully: This guy is always telling all the other voices to shut up.

It is a cathartic exercise to come up with names for the voices in your head. If you want to get more specific and name the critic in your head after your sophomore year English teacher, who we'll hypothetically call Ms. Anderson, it's even more fun. The point in the exercise is to create some detachment from the voices, which enables you to respond differently when they speak. There is more to you than the voices. *You are not the voices.* When you accept that, you can identify their patterns and when they speak the loudest, and you can respond with empathy.

I don't expect we will ever fully erase the negative voices in our internal soundtracks, but I believe we can slowly let other voices have greater influence over our thoughts and deeds. Loving, compassionate, tenderhearted, gentle voices, which normally speak so softly, become louder if we embrace God's call: "This is my beloved Son; listen to him!" When the internal voices start sounding more like Jesus and less like jerks, we are stepping into the abundance of the listening life.

LISTENING TO EMOTIONS

What was revolutionary about Ignatius's approach to discernment, and is still revolutionary in some Christian circles, is his assertion that emotions are to be taken seriously, even set in the center of our spirituality. For Ignatius, emotions are indicators of God's presence, or of God's felt absence. The "don't trust your emotions, trust God's Word" theology that prevails in some Christian circles would have been foreign to him.

Ignatius realized that the life of the Spirit, with its gifts of love, joy, peace and hope, has a strongly emotional content, and that is not something to be feared. A fear of or discomfort with emotions may lead us to overemphasize the intellectual aspects of faith, not to mention place a disproportional trust in the powers of our minds to apprehend the deep things of God. If we are new creatures, with fresh life continuously Spirit-breathed into us, then doesn't that mean that our emotions are also being redeemed, rescued from unbridled "passions" and transformed into healthy indicators of God's presence and our own internal states? When the two disciples who walked to Emmaus reflected on their night with that oddly familiar stranger, they marveled that their hearts burned within their chests as he spoke. A central part of the Christian spiritual life, then, comes in paying attention to the moments when our hearts are burning. In those times, we just may find that we are not alone.

As much as we post-Enlightenment types would like to claim the primacy of the intellect, humans are creatures ruled by emotions. We are the species with the most developed brains, yet our cerebral cortexes, which control the rational-thinking parts of our brains, are always playing catch up with the older, emotional-reacting parts of our brains. Our emotions move us to act and choose, and then our minds try to figure out why. It doesn't mean that we are helplessly captive to our emotions, but it does mean that we cannot discount the monumental role that emotions play in our lives and faith. Emotions are internal indicators of how we are doing and what is right, and what is wrong, with our circumstances and relationships. They motivate us to act and make decisions. They are God-given gauges of the state of our hearts and souls. Trying to ignore our feelings or push through them is not a healthy or mature perspective. Psychological studies reveal that emotional intelligence (EQ), our ability to understand and respond appropriately to our emotions and those of others, is more important for life success than IQ.

We ought to listen to our emotions before we start preaching to them. Let's not tell them what to do before they tell us what they are already doing. There is a time to weep, a time to laugh, a time to mourn and a time to dance. It's okay to not be okay. It feels like people, and advertisements, are constantly telling us what to feel or not feel. Scolding ourselves for being irrational or telling ourselves what we should be feeling is counterproductive. "Shoulds" almost always get in the way of genuine listening. Instead, let's allow our feelings to come and go as they will, without judging them, whitewashing them or correcting them.

Some Christians almost seem to view emotions as the voice of the tempter in the wilderness. If they are not silenced, they will lead you astray. I'm going out on a limb here to say that the voices of your emotions are *not* the voice of Satan. If you do happen to have a conversation with Satan himself, feel free to drop some Scripture on him and send the voice back to the hell from whence he came. I don't think Jesus' experience in the desert is meant to be an image of everyday emotional life. Your feeling of fear or anger is not the devil. Listening to your fear is different from letting your fear speak for you. You don't need to stretch out your feeling on a surgical table and cut it off. If you do, you're going to end up amputating your heart.

Most of our discernment work will involve sorting through the internal voices of our emotions and emotionally loaded thoughts. We listen to our emotions and name them. Those of us who are more at home in our heads than in our hearts, and who may find ourselves responding to questions about our feelings with our thoughts about our feelings, do well to simplify this process.

One therapist friend recommends talking about emotions in basic, childlike ways in order to penetrate our complicated adult defense mechanisms. The five core feelings—happiness, sadness, anger, fear and shame—get expressed as "glad," "sad," "mad," "scared" and "hurt." As part of my ministry training, for several months I sat in a small group and we shared gems like "When my supervisor disagreed with what I did, I felt mad," or "When the old man criticized my sermon, I felt hurt." (That last one was a universal experience for all the preachers in the room.)[11] Sometimes it felt pretty silly. Yet I was the youngest person in that group by at least fifteen years, and it struck me how people twenty to thirty years my senior struggled to understand and express their most basic emotions. Sometimes those of us with gifts for words develop those gifts as ways of concealing the emotions we have stifled since we were children.

One of the best motives for learning how to listen to your emotions, even if it requires some embarrassing conversations, is another emotion: relief. If you can put the right word to a feeling you are experiencing, your body will notice. Deborah van Duesen Hunsinger recommends an exercise called "focusing," in which you sit in the quiet and spend some time with an experience you have had or something that is troubling you.[12] As you reflect on it, you notice what is taking place in your body—usually you will notice some tightness or nervous energy or a pit in your stomach—and then you try to find the right word to describe what you are feeling. You shuffle through different words and pay attention to how your body responds; when you find the right name for your emotion, your body will relax and let out a deep breath.

It's enjoyable to watch other people have that experience in a conversation. I was spiritual director to a man who was wrestling with some issues with his aging parents. He was cycling through the same thoughts and problems in his mind without arriving at any satisfying solutions. My response to him was boringly simple. I said, "It sounds like your family situation is making you feel deeply anxious." That one isn't going to make any lists of inspirational quotes. But when I said the word *anxious*, his countenance changed. His shoulders slumped (high and tight shoulders often indicate anxiety), his eyes brightened, he released a deep sigh and his whole body relaxed. Once freed from the paralyzing effect of extreme anxiety, he was able to make a decision.

GREETING OUR EMOTIONS

We listen to our emotions best when we dialogue with ourselves. The first aspect of this self-dialogue simply involves acknowledging a feeling when it arises. You say hello to it. I have honestly had moments in my inner world when I said, *Well hello there, anxiety.* This is especially helpful when you are in the middle of a conversation with someone else and a feeling chimes in. By silently greeting the anxiety or hurt or anger that arises, or by noticing the subtle shift in your body even if you can't put words to it yet, you disarm some of its power in the moment and you become less likely to speak or act out of it. This is how you can avoid being reactive. You are not focusing on it in this moment, nor laboring to dismiss or silence it. You are noticing it, giving it a quick listen. Working to muzzle the emotion or condemning yourself for having it is focusing on it. Instead give the feeling a friendly hello and then return to the conversation at hand.

Afterward, you can explore the feeling that arose more thoroughly, either on your own or with a friend or therapist. Now is the time you can give the feeling, impulse or reaction that arose a deep listen by asking questions of it:

- When in the conversation or experience did the emotion arise? What exactly brought it out? What did the other person say or do?

- What was the feeling that I experienced? How would I name it (or them)? Anger, hurt, disappointment, shame, etc.?

- How did my body react to that emotion?

- How intensely did I feel it?

- Do I feel it often?

- Why did I feel it in that moment? How did I respond?

- Is there a word or a memory attached to that feeling?

- What is the source of the feeling? When else in my life do I remember feeling that emotion?

Listening to emotions is not a science or a checklist. The basic idea is to get to the source of the emotion and gain some understanding about why you feel the way you do. It's not easy; emotions have varying degrees of intensity and shades of meaning, and can come from very old and painful places. Getting to the deeper layers is a challenge. Further, emotions themselves have layers underneath them. They are indicators, pointing at something beyond themselves, namely, *needs*. Negative emotions indicate an unmet need. In every negative feeling, there is a positive need behind it.

Hunsinger says that in both listening to others and listening to ourselves, identifying the feeling is insufficient. We must explore the feeling and locate the *need* underneath it. For example, "Simply identifying the feeling of loneliness doesn't give one enough information to be able to take action. Compassionate exploration of the loneliness would identify the precise need underlying the loneliness."[13] Then the need underneath the emotion becomes a catalyst for taking action to address that need.

Anger is an especially difficult emotion for people to deal with constructively, particularly when they have been taught by their families or churches that anger is a sin. I seriously doubt that Jesus overturned the temple tables with a serene religious smile on his face. I learned a few years ago about the AHEN principle. AHEN: Anger comes from a Hurt, which comes from an Expectation, which comes from a Need.[14] Anger is a strong, protective emotion that can help us through a difficult situation. But it's also what's called a "presenting emotion," meaning that it often shows itself first but underneath it are more vulnerable emotions, like hurt or sadness. Anger shields us from those more exposed emotions until we are in a safer place.

Anger's second purpose is to usher us into the deep emotions underneath it and to give us clues as to how we can be healed. In order to dig underneath, you must able to say to yourself, *I am angry*. You want to feel the anger without letting it consume you, which you can do if you let it usher you into the deeper, scarier emotions and needs underneath it. Again, this is a matter of asking your anger questions and listening to its responses. The AHEN principle helps shape your questions. For example, if you find yourself angry at your spouse for being regularly late, you can work through it like this:

- What am I feeling? Angry.

- What is the hurt beneath the anger? I feel less important than her work.

- What is the expectation beneath the hurt? I expect to be more important than her job.

- What is the need beneath the expectation? I need to feel valued and loved.

This way you have let your anger serve its purpose and work for you. You don't get stuck in it, rehearsing the ways you have been wronged over and over again. And once you have worked your way down into your deep needs, you can take action to address the issue. You will find it much easier to have a conversation with the other person about it at that point. Conversations about needs are far more productive than conversations about anger.

Even our unhealthy behaviors and patterns indicate an unmet need. Christians, especially in more conservative circles, devote a lot of energy to "cutting off" sin. This language is often directed toward sexuality, particularly our need to "cut off" sexual desire. The intention is noble, but often the energy is misdirected. It's akin to the story of the Greek mythology hero Heracles, who discovered that every time he chopped off the head of the monstrous serpent Hydra, two more heads grew back in its place. We dedicate all our energy to suppressing desire, which usually only multiplies it. If someone tells you not to think about a unicorn, you're going to think about a unicorn. What we don't do is let our desires teach us and direct us to their source. There is a logic to sin; individual patterns and behaviors are not haphazard. They indicate an absence of the good in our lives, a void, an unmet need. Misplaced sexual desire or addiction usually indicates loneliness, which may point to broken relationships, unresolved pain, unfulfilled needs for love and acceptance, or simply an absence of good friendships. Sometimes if you give your sin a deep listen you might discover the key to truly cutting it off.

LISTENING TO YOUR BODY

I realize that the phrase "listen to your body" may make some Christians recoil in horror, but I would like to point out that recoiling is a bodily response, and you should probably listen to it. It is impossible for us to listen to our emotions without listening to our bodies, because it is in our bodies that we experience emotion. The pit in your stomach, the tightness in your shoulders, the lightness in your face, the heaviness in your eyelids, the sweaty palms—those are all clear physical indications of emotions. So if we are cut off from our bodies, we will be cut off from our feelings as well.

One of the more memorable conversations I have had was with my friend Jacqueline, who described an unusual therapy session. She and her therapist had been working through her views of her body, without much breakthrough. So her therapist got creative: she had Jacqueline sit in one chair and then placed an empty chair in front of her, telling Jacqueline to imagine that her body was sitting in it. She then instructed Jacqueline to talk to her body and to listen for what her body said in response. She told me, "It was incredibly weird, but nothing else had worked so I gave it a try. I then said a few things to my body. And do you know what my body had to say in response? Nothing. My body had absolutely nothing to say." She concluded that, out of self-hatred, she had spent years silencing and ignoring her body. Her body had lost its voice, and she was separated from a significant part of herself.

I read recently that Americans have less tolerance for hunger than any other civilization in history. We eat huge portions and snack throughout the day to avoid ever having to feel hungry, because even slight hunger causes us undue angst and mood fluctuation. A significant cause of the obesity problem in our country, which is also a huge issue among clergy, is that we don't know how to listen to what our bodies need and don't need. We don't know when we are supposed to eat and when we are not. Impulses and emotional cravings tend to dictate when and what we eat. We are deaf to our bodies' true signals. This isn't simply a health issue; this is also a spiritual issue. More and more I am convinced that if you want to know the state of your soul, pay attention to how you eat and drink.

When you resolve to eat healthier and eat less, you may discover previously buried sadness or other hidden emotions within you. That's one of the reasons Christians have fasted over the centuries; fasting is God-directed, but when you fast you also can no longer ignore the state of your internal world. You can't placate the wild animals snapping inside of you by throwing food at them; you must face them. Richard Foster said that when he spends extended time in fasting, he often discovers the things that control him.[15] Fasting is another way of amplifying the voices.

Our inability, or unwillingness, to hear our body's signals derives from the sharp line we often draw between the body and the spirit. We are tempted to consider the life of the body as secondary to developing an ungrounded life of the soul. The spirit is the realm of God, prayer the language of the angels, and the body is the realm of mere necessity, nagging appetites that distract from our truest work. We might roll our eyes at conversations about "basic" things like food or sleep, so we can focus on topics of more "gravity" like prayer or mission or how to read the Bible. The great Christian spiritual tradition, however, has always pivoted around incarnation and resurrection, the scandalous notion that God in Jesus has taken a human body and lived as a breathing, eating, walking human being. The entire human person has always been the arena for God's transforming work. Psychology professor David Benner says, "To be human is to be embodied, so any spirituality that fails to take the body seriously necessarily diminishes our humanity."[16] Spirituality that follows the pattern of Jesus will involve receiving the life of God into our ordinary, everyday, embodied human lives in anticipation of the day when our bodies will be fully renewed and glorified.

Some of us don't learn to listen to our bodies until the volume is turned up so loud that we can't ignore it any longer—namely, when we feel pain. Ideally, you don't want to wait until your hand touches the hot burner before you pay attention to your body's signals, but often that's the way it seems to go. Physical injury or severe heartbreak grabs our attention and reminds us just how intertwined our emotions, souls and bodies are. In the scourge and the serendipity of getting older we begin to notice the rhythms, movements, creaks and weaknesses of our bodies. I am not sure at what moment a person's response to the question "How are you?" shifts from "Fine!" to "Well, my arthritis is acting up and my back has been hurting . . ." but it would seem that that moment comes for everyone. I'll get back to you. The point is that when we get a little older our bodies start talking more, giving us more opportunities to listen. At a certain point our bodies force us to start listening, so I suggest that we start listening when it's still a choice.

My college roommate Sean didn't realize how tired he was until he was laid off from his law firm. He had been working sixty hours a week for months, and when he wasn't at the firm his brain was still working: on the car ride home, at the dinner table, in the middle of the night. He fought to keep his position, but the recession fell on him, just as it did so many others, like a guillotine. The afternoon after losing his position, he became reacquainted with his couch. After just a few moments of sitting still, he realized just how exhausted he was. He was flattened not only by a physical tiredness but by an emotional, mental, even spiritual tiredness— the kind of tired you get when you devote all your energy to something that doesn't give anything back, like blowing up a balloon with a tiny hole in it.

Ruth Haley Barton calls this a "dangerous" level of fatigue.[17] It's the point when you are so tired that you don't even realize it. The point when doubts and anger, rushing and out-of-character behavior start to creep in, but you don't know why. You just know that you don't feel completely at home in your body. In my experience as both a receiver of spiritual direction and a spiritual director to others, few professionals are as regularly and dangerously tired as pastors. Part of it is the nature of the work; unless you have done it you simply can't know how draining it is to help carry the spiritual, emotional and relational burdens of hundreds of people, not to mention write a decent sermon every week. More insidious are the theological justifications we give our exhaustion, when we actually *celebrate* how tired we are. The Son of Man had no place to lay his head, so there is no room for me to rest either! Whenever you start hearing phrases in a church like "burn out for Jesus," be very suspicious. It's okay to be "on fire for God" and still be well rested.

We do not glory in exhaustion, but those moments of dangerous tired force us to give an honest and sober listen to what our body is telling us. Listening to our bodies, just like listening to our emotions, involves asking good questions. Here are some places to start:

- What or who gives me energy? What or who drains my energy?

- When do I feel most alive? When do I feel most exhausted?

- What makes me feel rested? How much sleep do I need?

- When is my body most alert for prayer? Are there physical actions or postures that help me pray?

- What food makes me feel light and energized? What food makes me feel heavy and lethargic?

- What are my daily bodily rhythms? What time of the day do I have the most energy? The least? How do I tailor the various components of my life to work with those rhythms?

- What or who am I attracted to? What or who do I have a resistance to? Why?

The last questions derive from an emphasis in Ignatian spirituality on "attractions" and "repulsions," which Ignatius held were bodily indications of God's guidance in our lives. Especially in decision making, we ought to listen to what our body says as we entertain different options. If the fruit of the Spirit is peace and love, then God's calls to action will be accompanied by a sense of peace and love. I'm not fully convinced of that, since God's call to many of the prophets seemed to be accompanied by terror and loathing. But as a general rule, when we experience peace in our bodies, especially as we contemplate a hard decision, it is a strong indication of God's leading. If we feel a strong attraction to one option and a resistance to another, no matter how hard we try to convince ourselves of the opposite, we can begin to trust the magnetic pull of our bodies.[18] So often we drive ourselves crazy by turning over a problem in our mind again and again and again when our body already knows the answer.

LISTENING TO OUR SCRIPTS

Part of learning to discern the voices is noticing what can be called scripts, guiding stories about our identities and destinies that play through our head like movies. These are internal narratives, often unexamined, about who we are, how our lives should go, what we deserve, even what God is like. Scripts often get written at an early age, as authority figures tell us what we are like, what our strengths and weaknesses are, who our friends and enemies are, and how we will find success and happiness in life. Some of these stories are good and true, and others are not. Unfortunately, it is usually the scripts full of holes and lies that carry the most power. We get them stuck in our heads like bad songs:

- I'm loved only when I am good.

- Money will provide me the security that I need.

- I must do what others expect of me in order to be successful.

- I will only be truly happy when I'm married with children.

- My worth is in taking care of other people.

Pastoral consultant John Savage gives another example of a disastrous script: "When a child is told that he/she is stupid, dumb, or an idiot, and these words are repeated again and again, there is a very good chance that the receiver of these commands will begin to believe them and internalize them."[19] And that person may spend the rest of his life living according to that belief, or else desperately trying to prove that he's not stupid. He may expect others to confirm that message and thus interpret what they say and do through that script, regardless of what they intend.

After years of therapy I can now admit, reluctantly, that I was partly drawn to pastoral ministry because of the script running though my head that I'm not good enough. I know I'm not alone in that journey. We of course acknowledge the call of God that prevails over our compensating motivations, but those of us attracted to ministry, especially at a young age, are often driven by deep feelings of inadequacy. After all, who is more worthy than a minister? If I succeed as a pastor, then I will finally be okay, right? Maybe if I can rescue others from their pain, then I will find the solution for my own. If I can impress masses of people, then I'll finally win the approval of my parents. In the beginning stages, the attention and admiration you receive in ministry feels validating, but once you rediscover your numerous inadequacies (and it doesn't take long), disillusionment, doubt and burnout often occur. Even the most lavish praise from your congregation will never heal your wounds or rewrite your scripts.

False scripts are what Jesus encountered in the wilderness, just like Adam and Eve and Israel before him. We're not given details about how exactly the adversary "appears" to Jesus, but one possibility is that he speaks as a voice in Jesus' head. The tempter offers him narratives about who he is and what shape the reign of the Messiah should assume. The Son of God should rule with power and glamour and eat the finest cuisine in all the land. Subtext: You certainly shouldn't be a humble servant, drink from the cup of suffering and die on a cross.

Jesus' temptation script directly contradicts the baptism script given in the previous scene. There, before he had begun his ministry or done anything of note, Jesus hears a different voice: "You are my Son, the Beloved; with you I am well pleased." The temptation script shouts: "You must prove that you are beloved, silence the doubters who don't believe you're God's Son and provide for yourself." The baptism script whispers: "You are beloved in this moment, you can rest in the identity God has given you, and God will provide." Jesus, and each one of us, must decide which script we will listen to. Do I believe I am God's beloved, or that I must prove that I am God's beloved? Our first ancestors decided that God was withholding from them. Jesus decided that he had everything he needed.

LISTENING FOR THE QUESTIONS

You can't have a vocation unless you are a listener. *Vocation* is from the Latin word for "calling," and a calling requires both a caller and a listener. To say that you have a vocation is to say that a voice has moved you, that something deeper than personal advancement or interest has summoned you.

Conversations about calling too quickly become conversations about career, as though your career is your calling wrapped up in a 401(k). It has been a luxury of modern life and of Christendom to be able to pursue vocation on a professional level, when even the apostle Paul was making tents to bring the gospel to the Gentiles. I suspect that as fewer and fewer people set their watches by church bells, more and more Christian workers will need to support their calling through outside work. We can't expect the economy to pay us for following Jesus' voice. It was nice while it lasted though.

There was a time when I thought that finding my vocation meant discovering the answers and gifts that I have for the world's problems and deficiencies. I would know my calling when I stumbled upon what I could fix and who I could rescue. Ask me how well that worked out. I now believe that my calling is not the answers but the questions that I bring to the world. Perhaps the caller gives us questions, and perhaps our pursuit of vocation will mean listening for the questions.

As Rainer Maria Rilke famously said, "Be patient toward all that is unsolved in your heart and try to love the questions themselves, like locked rooms and like books that are now written in a very foreign tongue. Do not now seek the answers, which cannot be given you because you would not be able to live them. And the point is, to live everything. Live the questions now."[20] Answers are too often held in a closed fist, fingers wrapped tightly around them. They can isolate us and keep us in the same place, leaving us wondering why no else is coming to us and our conclusions. Questions balance on the tips of your outstretched fingers, open and welcoming, inviting fresh possibilities and refinement. Questions move you toward the world and toward community, drawing others into them and you into theirs.

I once heard an executive of a global nonprofit organization say that their mission statement was "the kind of mission statement that gets you up in the morning." I am searching for the questions that get me up in the morning. I want the questions to occasionally keep me up at night. I want to live and love the questions. I want my life to be a living question.

People will try to tell us what our questions should be, which will usually be *their* questions. We can save ourselves much anxiety and energy by devoting ourselves to our questions, rather than trying to ask the questions we "should" ask. There is no hierarchy of questions. Your questions are profoundly personal and must be fired from your soul. The questions are soul deep, and you will know when you stumble on them because they will fill you with a driving passion that you have no idea what to do with.

Our vocational questions will be broad and searching, transcending the essential and everyday questions of personal survival. How do I feed myself? is a survival question. How do I address the unjust distribution of healthy food in my community? is a vocational question. We listen for the questions that are far reaching, usually just out of our reach, God-oriented but not necessarily religious, motivated by love, requiring faith, and steeped in hope.

Your questions will reflect your personality. My questions will probably be hopelessly abstract, because nothing bores me faster than the practical. People who exult in practical questions will get a lot more done than I do.

The question that seemed to get Jesus up in the morning was "How do I usher in the kingdom of God on earth?" This was his life question, and it drove him everywhere he went, from holy houses to disreputable homes, from the head of the table to the least of all. The right questions sweep you up and take you to new places and new people, moving you forward into risk, compelling you to keep going when you encounter obstacles.

What are the questions that get you up in the morning? My friend Jessica, a landscape architect, says that the question that drives her is "How do I design public spaces so that communities will thrive in them and people will come together?" Another friend who suffered abuse as a child asks, "How can I free abuse victims from shame and help them know that they are loveable?" A father asks, "How can I help my child to become her true self?" The question that drives me forward more than anything else now is "How do people change?" That question has compelled me into writing and into different ministries and into the ancient spiritual disciplines of the Christian tradition, not to mention personal therapy. I am driven to know how it is that we are transformed from one person to another, deeper and deeper into the image of Christ.

Your questions will be fluid, and they will change as you move through different phases of your life and relationships. I don't believe that we only receive one calling in our lifetime. Your questions as a mother of toddlers will be quite different from your questions after they have grown up and gotten married. A question that makes your heart burn at age thirty may be extinguished at age fifty. After all, Jesus was a carpenter until he was thirty. The questions we are given will change—they are the beginning of the chapter, not the end—which is why we must persist in listening for them in every phase of life.

LISTENING TO YOUR SCORE

Imagine that there was a composer so skilled and so intuitive that he could take your life and put it to music. He could write a score that captured the pace, the volume, the pitch, the rhythms, the crescendos and declines, and the alternating patterns of movement and rest in your life. Do you think the symphony he composed would be one that you would enjoy listening to?

I put that question to a group of people gathered for a weekend retreat, some of whom were professional classical musicians, and the conversation that followed was lively. Someone first asked, "What makes a piece of music great?" Many agreed that a great and enduring piece of music is complex, with varied themes, moving at different paces and playing at changing volumes. We wanted lives that played like great compositions, that though they would be as unique as each person would be worth listening to again and again, and that inspired people who heard them.

We also agreed that our lives played in rhythms that did not always make for good music. One person said that her life felt too dominated by staccato—short, separated notes—by which she meant that her life seemed to bounce from one quick activity to the next without any clear relationship between them. Many lamented that their personal and professional lives seemed to always play at fortissimo—very loud—and in fast time, the notes slurring together. Pretty much everyone agreed that they needed to break up their movements with more and longer rests. We longed for more piano—quiet—and more adagio—slow.

Ultimately, the score that our life plays is an echo of the voices that sound inside of us. Though we will all play in different ways, and different seasons of our lives will produce different rhythms, it is likely true that an overly loud and crowded outer life is an indication of an overly loud and crowded inner life. Or, an overly quiet and slow outer life may indicate some untreated wounds and fears inside of us as well. If we want to hear what is happening in us, we can start by listening to the rhythms and sounds in the outer lives we lead.

NINE

The Society of
Reverse Listening

OUR CHURCH SIGNS LAY OUT THE USUAL PATTERN. Come this Sunday for our message: "Where Is God When It Hurts?" This week's sermon: "Abraham and Isaac: The Untold Story." Sunday morning at 9 and 11: "Your One True Love." The expectation is clear: if you come to church, you are going to listen. The church's job is to preach, to teach the Bible and to share God's opinions on the issues of the day, and your job is to listen to our message. We have a pulpit, and you have ears.

Imagine if the pattern was reversed. What if, instead of coming to church to be preached to, people came to church to be heard? What if the body of believers was known less as a preaching community and more as a listening community? What if the church was a group of people where the power dynamics of speaking and listening were inverted? Imagine a society of reverse listening, where those who would normally expect to be heard, listen, and those who would normally expect to listen, are heard. I dream of a place where leaders listen to followers, adults listen to children, men listen to women, the majority listens to the minority, the rich listen to the poor, and insiders listen to outsiders.

If the church as the society of reverse listening could ever be realized, it would have to start with our leaders. When those on the top start to listen like those on the bottom, we're starting to live like Jesus. Sadly, for all our talk about servant leadership, I have not encountered many pastors and other Christian leaders who are devoted to listening. You don't get to be a celebrity pastor through listening, that's for certain. There is no money on the listening circuit. Too many of us seem to be in a hurry, and hurry and good listening are bitter enemies. Yet the first act of a servant leader is to listen, and the quality of listening in our churches will largely be determined by the level of commitment our leaders have to listening.

Four years ago, I interviewed for a church ministry position with college students and young adults. Here is how the conversation went:

Church Leaders: "What are the programs that you plan to implement if you take the position?"

Me: "Honestly, I don't like to come with an already established template that I plug in to a new place. I think that programs must flow organically from the particular community of people I would be working with. Because I don't know who the people are yet, I wouldn't want to impose programs on them that wouldn't fit them. So, my first task would be to take people out for coffee and ask questions and listen, to find out who they are and what the needs of the community are."

Church Leaders: "Um, okay. And exactly how long will that phase last?"

I didn't get the job.

When our communities are led by people who do not value listening, we may end up with ministries and structures that come from other contexts but are not suited to the actual people we lead. I have seen this often in new church plants. Well-meaning people import programs that were highly successful in another church into a new community, only to have it flounder. That wildly successful small group ministry in a suburban megachurch may not translate well to a small urban church in a diverse neighborhood. We must learn to listen locally, so that we are addressing the actual lives and needs of our people, not the people somewhere else. And we must not only listen once, as we undertake a new church plant or program, but we must keep listening, because our churches and neighborhoods are always changing.

THE COMMUNITY WHO LISTENS

My dream for the church is that we would be known as the community who listens. Our listening would be multidirectional; with one ear turned out and one ear turned in, our listening would be just as much a part of our mission as our pastoral care and church government.

Listening in. I was a part of a church community recently that held what they called "listening posts." Church leaders set up several open times in different neighborhoods for church members to come and share their hopes for and frustrations about the church. The sole job of the pastors and elders was to listen and ask questions. They were careful not to set an agenda for each listening post, giving people the opportunity to share whatever they wanted to share. I don't remember any particular conclusions and directions taken as a result of the listening posts, and in retrospect, I think that was the point. Listening was an end in itself. Listening, on the part of the pastors and elders, was a way of showing openness, humility and a submission to the Holy Spirit speaking through the church as a whole. The listening posts were means for showing love and respect for the people of the church, a way of acknowledging each person's role in community and ministry and the value of each individual voice.

It also occurred to me how rare that sort of church listening is, and how unfortunate it is that we have to set up special meetings in order for people to feel heard. This sort of listening, where the normal direction of listening is reversed, is an indispensable element for our people and churches to grow into the image of Christ, the listening expression of Jesus' upside-down kingdom. I think of Jesus putting a child in the midst of the crowd and saying, "Whoever does not receive the kingdom of God as a little child will never enter it" (Mark 10:15). This is his summons for adults to listen to children, to not only call them up to the front to preach a children's sermon to them but to let them preach their sermons to us.

I think about Jesus' interaction with the Samaritan woman outside of town at the well as his call for men to listen to women, insiders to listen to outsiders, reversing destructive cultural trends. Or consider James's exhortation that if a wealthy and well-dressed person walks into your sanctuary and you give him the seat of honor while telling the person in shabby clothes to sit at your feet, you show an unjust partiality. Instead, we give up our seats for the poor, the disheveled, the outcasts, the outliers, those who look different from us, and we sit at their feet and listen to them. We let them teach us. As has been said, it is not that certain people in our society lack a voice; rather it is that they lack listeners.

Listening for unity. The call to unity rings loud through churches of all sizes and traditions, but what exactly makes for church unity? Many claim that unity comes from shared belief, but those communities that press the hardest for common doctrine too often draw sharp lines between insiders—those who believe everything we do—and outsiders—those who disagree or, as usually interpreted, those who are wrong. It may begin as a line that starts at the church door, dividing believers from unbelievers, but eventually that line starts creeping its way into the church itself, dividing true believers from false believers.

We find ourselves retreating into echo chambers, where the voices around us sound just like ours, saying our words out of another mouth. This reflects a larger cultural trend. An important book called *The Big Sort*, by Bill Bishop, demonstrates how Americans are increasingly clustering into neighborhoods where we are surrounded by people who think, act and vote like we do. Our country is becoming more and more polarized, both culturally and geographically, and our churches seem to be following a similar monocultural trend. We are not just turning a deaf ear toward those with different experiences or perspectives; we don't even have to hear them in the first place.

While this is an alarming trend, I'm still not convinced that communities that appear homogenous on the outside are as alike as they seem. I suspect, or I'll even go so far as to say I *know*, that our churches are filled with people who have a range of political, theological and social opinions. The first issue may not be a lack of diversity but a lack of tolerance for diversity, an inability to listen to people say things that we may not agree with or like. There are many who remain silent in our communities, often with resentment bubbling beneath the surface, in order to keep the peace, either because they want to avoid conflict or because they fear the consequences of speaking up. Needless to say, we will not have communities who listen as long as people fear punishment for possessing alternative opinions.

When the New Testament speaks of unity, the vast majority of the time it does not speak of perfect doctrinal agreement. It speaks of love. What unites us in the church is love, flowing between us through the power of the Holy Spirit. When we listen to one another, and give others permission to be their own person and think their own thoughts, we love one another.

It has always been my hope to hear a pastor stand up in front of a worshiping community and say something like "We are the body of Christ, the children of God, the beloved of the Holy Spirit. That does not mean that we are all the same. We are not. We think differently. We experience feelings differently. We have different experiences and perspectives and pasts and hopes for the future. We vote in elections differently. We read the Bible in different ways. We even understand God differently. We as a church are rooted in the great Christian tradition and the creeds the church around the world has affirmed for millennia, but we honor that people are coming from different places and moving at different paces. We honor the questions and the doubts and the struggles that everyone has, and we will never try to silence them or dismiss them. What bonds us together is love, and love's only demand is that you be yourself. Our goal is unity, not uniformity, and we aim for genuine community, not artificial conformity. That means that we will disagree, sometimes bitterly, but we will stay at the table and keep listening to those we disagree with. Our unity is in our commitment to listen to one another."

Listening out. It was a privilege of Christendom that we could have a reasonable expectation that people would listen to our message, or at least pretend they were listening. In an age when the church has lost some of its influence and prestige, our temptation may be to turn up our volume. Backed into a corner, feeling like a persecuted minority, we might fight harder and preach louder. We hope that our shouting will unplug the ears of a culture that has ceased to listen to us. Instead, I consider this a good time for the church to listen. Once an army of preachers, we can now put people on the front lines of listening. Our relative loss of power is an opportunity for us to learn what our neighbors and culture value and want. Instead of being the People With Answers, we can discover what questions others are actually asking. This is an age where the church has to earn the right to be heard, and I know of no better way to do that than to listen first.

EARS TO THE GROUND

Scot McKnight told me that he thinks the most effective Christian communities are those who "have their ears to the ground," listening to the movements of the surrounding culture.[1] After all, in order to be able to love our neighbors, we have to know who they are.

In college I had the opportunity to participate in two urban churches thirty miles east of Los Angeles. Five miles apart, they were part of the same larger community, but their relationships to their neighborhoods could not have been more different. Over the previous fifty years, the city had undergone significant transition. Once predominately Caucasian, the vast majority of households were now Hispanic. Both congregations, once thriving, dwindled as members moved out of the neighborhood into nearby suburbs, and they struggled to know how to adjust to the new demographics of the area.

The two churches responded to this migration in dramatically different ways. One church turned inward, ignoring the cultural change around it, and became all but irrelevant to its neighbors. Its remaining members commuted in from the suburbs they had escaped to, only driving through the church neighborhood on their way to and from the freeway. As lovely as those people were, they had little interest in extending hospitality to newcomers or finding points of intersection with their immediate neighbors. Today, the church has fifteen people attending weekly worship, and it is one of those sad cases where the governing body is waiting for the members to die so they can sell the property.

The second congregation, a little north and in a more populated area, took a different approach. They sent members out to do a survey of the neighborhood, partly for information gathering but mostly to meet their neighbors. They wanted to know who they were, what they needed, what they cared about and how they struggled. In other words, they listened. And what they heard changed them and the nature of their ministry. The first need that surfaced was a safe place for children to go after school. The church launched an afterschool tutoring program, recruiting some students from nearby colleges to help, which is how I was introduced to the church. The tutoring program eventually grew into a community center for mentoring, advocacy and community organizing. Now members of the church and of the immediate and broader neighborhoods teach classes for both children and parents, offer job training and employment opportunities, and run a cooperative garden and computer center.[2]

Today the church, while still small, has a multiethnic and multilingual worshiping community—because they chose to turn their ear toward their community and listen.

LISTENING TO YOUR COMMUNITY'S STORY

I had the opportunity recently to do a community walk in an urban Los Angeles neighborhood with Michael Mata, urban development director for World Vision US. Mata regularly takes groups of people on neighborhood walks, teaching them how to assess the structures and symbols of a community. This is a practice that can be easily translated to a variety of communities and something that churches and other Christian groups could practice often. This is the spiritual discipline of the long community walk. It is an exercise in people listening together for the story that their community is telling.

What you do is walk through your neighborhood as a small group and ask questions of what you are noticing and experiencing. Mata had us ask questions like these:

- How is space used? Is there a sense that people are welcome here? Are there sidewalks or bike lanes? Are there bars on the windows or high gates or hedges?

- What kinds of homes do people live in? How are they kept up? How many people are living in the average home or apartment?

- What political signs do you notice? Billboards? What are their messages? What might they reveal about who lives here, how they vote and what they buy?

- What do you hear? What languages are people speaking? Do you hear children playing or crying?

- What kinds of vehicles do you see?

- What kinds of symbols do you notice? Religious, economic, political?

- Who do you see? What are their ages? Ethnic backgrounds? Socioeconomic status?

- Who are the authority figures here? Are there police? Is their presence welcome or unwelcome?

If you listen well, what you hear in each neighborhood will be unique. What you hear in a lower-class urban neighborhood will obviously be quite different from what you hear in an upper-class suburb, but these questions can be asked in any context with some adjustment. The process of listening together is just as important as the conclusions your group draws.

Most important, Mata insisted that we look not only for

problems in the community but for signs of hope. In certain neighborhoods it is easy to collapse into despair at the number of problems and tensions that you observe. But he had us listen for the resources, the gifts, the possibilities, the strengths of the community, even if we had to get imaginative with them. For example, a vacant lot has potential for a meeting space, a park or a community garden. As we talked about what resources can be nurtured or cultivated in a community, I thought about the apostle Paul in Athens, observing the religious idols in the city and especially the one dedicated to an "unknown god." Paul both grieved the religious confusion in the city and saw that particular statue as an opportunity to preach Christ. He heard the Athenian longing for God and for knowledge of the big powers of the universe. Listening to our communities will involve grieving and identifying with their pain but also finding signs of hope, openness and spiritual desire in our neighborhoods. As missiologist Michael Frost put it, "Listen to your neighborhood. They are telling you how to heal them."[3]

The needs of our churches, cities and neighborhoods can be staggering. When we view the problems of our world from a distance, we may feel paralyzed and helpless. Further, with lives already overloaded with busyness we are reluctant to add more activities. Proximity is the key. There are nameless, faceless voices, and then there is the person right in front of you. Mother Teresa once said, "Never worry about numbers. Help one person at a time and always start with the person nearest you." You don't have to go to the ends of the earth to listen for the needs of others. If you are unsure what to do and who to help, listen to the person nearest you. Wherever you are. And prepare to be changed by what you hear.

Epilogue

LISTENING GOES LAST. When I worked in hospice, I always told families to keep talking to patients, because no matter how unresponsive they seemed, they could still hear. On a deep level, as deep as the soul, people on the brink of eternity could hear the whispers and songs of love their families offered them as parting gifts.

Listening is the first thing we do in life, and it is the last thing we do in death. We don't have a choice then, but we do have a choice for all the points in between. The honest truth is that there is no glory in listening. There is more glory in talking about listening than there is in actually doing it. It is the New Year's resolution of relationship disciplines. It is not glamorous, charismatic or dynamic. People who have been heard well aren't even aware of it half the time.

Yet when you commit to go deep into listening, you will find that listening "speaks" in ways far more powerful than talking ever could. The most profound sermon, masterfully delivered, cannot compare to the experience of being truly heard. People don't line up at the sanctuary door to shake your hand after you have listened, but ten thousand true and beautiful words cannot convey love like unhurried listening.

Listening is a gift. It is a gift from God to us that sparks intimacy, that helps us grow into servants and disciples, that promises constant learning and self-discovery, that helps us never lose the childlike gift of being surprised, and that assures us of guidance and the awareness of God's presence. It is a gift that God offers—in the staggering discovery that God actually listens to us—and it is a gift that we offer others, an open invitation to receive whatever they choose to share with us.

Will you embrace the gift of listening?

Notes

INTRODUCTION

[1]David Benner, *Sacred Companions: The Gift of Spiritual Friendship and Direction* (Downers Grove, IL: InterVarsity Press, 2004), 158.

[2]John Gray, *Men Are from Mars, Women Are from Venus* (New York: HarperCollins, 1992).

1: THE LISTENING LIFE

[1]Quote recorded by one of Hendricks's students, Dale Burke, at http://seacoast-church.org/howard-hendricks-quotes.

[2]Shane Hipps, *The Hidden Power of Electronic Culture* (Grand Rapids: Zondervan, 2005), 71.

[3]Seth S. Horowitz, "The Science and Art of Listening," *The New York Times*, November 9, 2012, http://mobile.nytimes.com/2012/11/11/opinion/sunday/why-listening-is-so-much-more-than-hearing.html?_r=0.

[4]Don Ihde, *Listening and Voice: Phenomenologies of Sound* (Albany: State University of New York Press, 2007), 81.

[5]John M. Gottman, *The Seven Principles for Making Marriage Work* (New York: Harmony Publishers, 2000), 45.

[6]Scot McKnight, *The Blue Parakeet: Rethinking How You Read the Bible* (Grand Rapids: Zondervan, 2008), 98.

[7]Louise Story, "Anywhere the Eye Can See, It's Likely to See an Ad," *The New York Times*, January 15, 2007, www.nytimes.com/2007/01/15/business/media/15everywhere.html?pagewanted=1&_r=0.

[8]Christine Rosen, "The Myth of Multitasking," *The New Atlantis*, no. 20 (Spring 2008): 105-10, available online at www.thenewatlantis.com/publications/the-myth-of-multitasking.

[9]Kendall Paladino, "Mother Teresa Saw Loneliness as Leprosy of the

West," *The News-Times (Danbury, CT),* April 17, 2004, www.newstimes
.com/news/article/Mother-Teresa-saw-loneliness-as-leprosy-of
-the-250607.php.

[10]Referenced in Rosen, "The Myth of Multitasking," www.thenewatlantis
.com/publications/the-myth-of-multitasking.

[11]See Skye Jethani, *The Divine Commodity* (Grand Rapids: Zondervan, 2009),
47-52.

[12]Quoted in Idhe, *Listening and Voice*, 7.

[13]Ibid.

[14]Walter Ong, *Orality and Literacy* (New York: Routledge, 1982), 71.

[15]Hipps, *Hidden Power of Electronic Culture*, 71.

2: THE KING WHO LISTENS

[1]Edward Hickman, ed., *Works of Jonathan Edwards*, vol. 2 (Edinburgh:
Banner of Truth Trust, 1974), 113.

[2]See Mother Teresa and Brian Kolodiejchuk, *Come Be My Light: The Private
Writings of the Saint of Calcutta* (New York: Image, 2009).

3: LISTENING TO GOD

[1]See Ruth Haley Barton's magnificent book *Invitation to Solitude and Silence*
(Downers Grove, IL: InterVarsity Press, 2010).

[2]See Willard's now classic book *Hearing God*, expanded ed. (Downers Grove,
IL: InterVarsity Press, 2012).

[3]Dallas Willard, *The Divine Conspiracy: Rediscovering Our Hidden Life in God*
(New York: Harper, 1998), 66.

[4]From the poem "Hound of Heaven" by Francis Thompson.

[5]This paragraph is a small summary of a great conversation I once had with
my Presbyterian pastor-friend Kirk Winslow.

[6]I swear that Thomas Merton said this somewhere, but for the life of me, I
can't find the source.

[7]From David Benner's book *Opening to God* (Downers Grove, IL: Inter-
Varsity Press, 2010), 26.

[8]Aslan sings Narnia into existence in *The Magician's Nephew.* What a crazy lion.

[9]Henri J. Nouwen, "Moving from Solitude to Community to Ministry,"
Leadership Journal, Spring 1995.

[10]Willard, *Hearing God*, 42.

[11]Quoted in Willard, *Hearing God*, 175-76.

[12]Henri Nouwen, *The Way of the Heart* (New York: HarperOne, 2009), 28.

[13]John Calvin, *Institutes of the Christian Religion*, vol. 1, ed. John T. McNeil, trans. Ford Lewis Battles (Louisville, KY: Westminster John Knox, 1960), 7.4.

[14]Willard, *Hearing God.*

[15]T. S. Eliot, "Ash Wednesday," in *The Complete Poems and Plays of T. S. Eliot* (London: Faber and Faber, 2004).

[16]Robert Gelinas, *Finding the Groove: Composing a Jazz-Shaped Faith* (Grand Rapids: Zondervan, 2009), 44. This Coltrane story largely comes out of Gelinas's outstanding book.

[17]Ibid., 45.

[18]Ibid. Consider putting your feet up tonight, turning on *A Love Supreme* and going deep into the night with the sound of God. *A Love Supreme* could change your life.

[19]Lewis Porter, *John Coltrane: His Life and Music* (Ann Arbor: University of Michigan Press, 2000), 232.

[20]Willard, *Hearing God*, 56; italics added. At this point you really have to be wondering why you are reading this book instead of his.

[21]Raging Waters Conference, Fuller Seminary, April 2011.

[22]I'm paraphrasing something Barth said in the *Church Dogmatics*. He said it with more eloquence and much more verbosity. I'm pretty sure right now he is with the Lord pounding out more volumes.

[23]Nowen, *The Way of the Heart*, 28.

[24]Quoted in Jerry Sittser, *The Will of God as a Way of Life: How to Make Every Decision with Peace and Confidence* (Grand Rapids: Zondervan, 2004), 87.

[25]Ibid., 90.

4: LISTENING TO SCRIPTURE

[1]Thanks to Susan Howatch for the phrase "glamorous powers" and for her entire Starbridge series, especially *Glittering Images*, which introduced me to spiritual direction. Plus, it's just a crazy ride.

[2]Michael Casey, *Sacred Reading: The Art of Lectio Divina* (Liguori, MO: Triumph Books, 1996), 58. The medicine chest analogy also comes from this work, 47.

[3]Eugene Peterson calls this heuristic writing in his *The Pastor: A Memoir* (New York: HarperOne, 2012), 239.

[4]Eugene Peterson, *Eat This Book: A Conversation in the Art of Spiritual Reading* (Grand Rapids: Eerdmans, 2009), 24.

[5]Chris Webb, *The Fire of the Word: Meeting God on Holy Ground* (Downers Grove, IL: InterVarsity Press, 2011), 60.

[6]Peterson, *Eat This Book*, 88.

[7]Scot McKnight, *The Blue Parakeet: Rethinking How You Read the Bible* (Grand Rapids: Zondervan, 2008), 41.

[8]Ibid., 89.

[9]Ibid, 96.

[10]Let's be honest: *Moby-Dick* could use a little *less* story. I started reading it when I was seventeen and I just finished it last week.

[11]See the excellent conversation on Ignatian prayer in Gary Neal Hansen's *Kneeling with Giants: Learning to Pray with History's Best Teachers* (Downers Grove, IL: InterVarsity Press, 2012).

[12]Peterson, *Eat This Book*, 91.

[13]Adele Calhoun's *Spiritual Disciplines Handbook: Practices That Transform Us* (Downers Grove, IL: InterVarsity Press, 2005) helped me to craft this method.

[14]Both quotes are from *Reading Scripture with the Church Fathers* (Downers Grove, IL: InterVarsity Press, 1998), 41.

[15]Peterson, *The Pastor*, 71.

5: LISTENING TO CREATION

[1]*Epistola* CVI, sect. 2, in *The Early English Church*, translation from Edward Churton (1840), 324.

[2]Calvin, *Institutes of the Christian Religion*, vol. 1, ed. John T. McNeil, trans. Ford Lewis Battles (Louisville, KY: Westminster John Knox, 1960), 72.

[3]Ibid., 179.

[4]Karl Barth said that Jesus Christ is "the key to the secret of creation," but I think Jesus is actually the secret himself. What does Karl Barth know? (Karl Barth, *The Doctrine of Creation* 3.1, *Church Dogmatics* [Edinburgh: T&T Clark, 2004]).

[5]Thanks to Leighton Ford for pointing out this connection of word and world and for the interpretation of the Magi story. Check out his excellent book *The Attentive Life: Discerning God's Presence in All Things* (Downers Grove, IL: InterVarsity Press, 2014).

[6]Augustine, *Confessions,* trans. R. S. Pine-Coffin (London: Penguin, 1961), bk. 10, chap. 6, 212.

[7]Richard Foster, *Sanctuary of the Soul: Journey into Meditative Prayer* (Downers Grove, IL: InterVarsity Press, 2011), 141.

[8]Quoted by Trent Gilliss, "On Beauty: Places to Play and Pray," *On Being,* October 6, 2013, www.onbeing.org/blog/on-beauty-places-to-play-and -pray/6015.

[9]In case you're wondering, when I take my glasses off on these contemplative strolls, I have only walked into the path of a moving car four or five times.

[10]Quoted in *A Jonathan Edwards Reader,* ed. John E. Smith, Harry S. Stout and Kenneth P. Minkema (New Haven, CT: Yale University Press, 2013), 7-8.

[11]Janna Levin, "The Sound the Universe Makes," TED Talk, March 2011, www.ted.com/talks/janna_levin_the_sound_the_universe_makes.html.

[12]Rob Bell, "Why We Should Care About Advent," *Relevant Magazine,* November 29, 2010, www.relevantmagazine.com/god/deeper-walk /features/23640-why-advent.

[13]Eugene Peterson, *Christ Plays in Ten Thousand Places: A Conversation in Spiritual Theology* (Grand Rapids: Eerdmans, 2008), 67-69. This whole section is highly influenced by this book. I am not smart enough to come up with this stuff by myself.

[14]Riffing on Peterson, "We wake up to a world we did not make" (ibid., 51).

[15]Rob Bell gave a great sermon on this at Mars Hill Bible Church, as part of a God Is Green series, and this section draws from his ideas but does not follow the weird spacing in his books.

[16]Also from the God Is Green sermon series.

[17]Ford, *The Attentive Life,* 22.

[18]See Phyllis Tickle's introduction to *The Divine Hours: Prayers for Summertime* (New York: Image, 2006). This is my favorite contemporary resource for praying the hours. And you know, there's also an app for that.

[19]Henri Nouwen, *A Cry for Mercy* (New York: Image, 2002), 43.

[20]I learned about this through Christine Valters Paintner's book *Water, Wind, Earth, and Fire: The Christian Practice of Praying with the Elements* (Notre Dame, IN: Sorin Publishers, 2010).

[21]I think I got this idea from an episode of *The West Wing* where there was a possible case of mad cow disease in the United States. It didn't end up being true, but Leo, C. J. and Jed had an hour-long conflict about it. It was good TV. Watch that show.

[22]From his book *The Problem of Pain* (New York: HarperCollins, 2014).

[23]The Green Bible (New York: Harper, 2006), I-36.

[24]Romans 8:22-23. The Greek root is *stenazo*, meaning to groan or to sigh.

[25]See the excellent publication of the National Association of Evangelicals, *Loving the Least of These*, www.nae.net/lovingtheleastofthese. I am happy that evangelicals are slowly coming to these realizations.

[26]John Vidal, "A Great Silence Is Being Spread Over the Natural World," *The Guardian*, September 3, 2012, http://m.guardian.co.uk/environment/2012 /sep/03/bernie-krause-natural-world-recordings?cat=environment&type =article.

6: LISTENING TO OTHERS

[1]I believe I first heard the phrase "listening to the hearts of those around me" in Norm Wakefield's book *Between the Words: The Art of Perceptive Listening* (Grand Rapids: Revell, 2002).

[2]The Hebrew rendering is *lev shema*.

[3]Deborah Van Deusen Hunsinger talks about this extensively in her book *Pray Without Ceasing: Revitalizing Pastoral Care* (Grand Rapids: Eerdmans, 2006).

[4]H. Jackson Brown, *The Complete Life's Little Instruction Book* (Nashville: Thomas Nelson, 2000), 116.

[5]I have seen that quote attributed to about 742 different people. But not St. Francis, surprisingly.

[6]Dietrich Bonhoeffer, *Life Together* (New York: HarperOne, 2009), 93.

[7]This happens less at Presbyterian churches.

[8]Apparently St. Francis did not write this prayer, and it didn't show up until early in the twentieth century. Why is it that every quote attributed to St. Francis is fake?

[9]Wakefield, *Between the Words*, 49.

[10]Tom Hamilton, in *East of Eden*, is the one who is said to have "a good ear." Later, he killed himself.

[11]Hunsinger, *Pray Without Ceasing*, 52.

7: LISTENING TO PEOPLE IN PAIN

[1]Dietrich Bonhoeffer, *Life Together* (New York: HarperOne, 2009), 97.

[2]Dr. Seuss may or may not have said this. The quote is widely attributed to him, with no specific source. St. Francis probably originally said it.

[3]Bonhoeffer, *Life Together*, 97.

[4]Read about this in depth in Daniel Goleman's *Social Intelligence: The New Science of Human Relationships* (New York: Bantam Books, 2006).

[5]Deborah Van Deusen Hunsinger has a great section on anxiety and listening in her book *Pray Without Ceasing: Revitalizing Pastoral Care* (Grand Rapids: Eerdmans, 2006), 80.

[6]William Ury, *Getting Past No* (New York: Bantam, 1993), 52.

[7]Hunsinger, in *Pray Without Ceasing*, 64, says, "When one focuses only on one's feelings and fails to identify the underlying needs, one can get ensnared in simply rehearsing how bad one feels."

8: LISTENING TO YOUR LIFE

[1]The phrase "Listen to your life" comes from Frederick Buechner, in a book titled—wait for it—*Listening to Your Life* (San Francisco: HarperSanFrancisco, 1992).

[2]Parker Palmer, *Let Your Life Speak: Listening for the Voice of Vocation* (San Franisco: Jossey-Bass, 1999), 4.

[3]Quoted in Ruth Haley Barton, *Invitation to Solitude and Silence: Experiencing God's Transforming Presence* (Downers Grove, IL: InterVarsity Press, 2010), 43.

[4]Madeleine L'Engle, *Walking on Water: Reflections on Faith and Art* (Colorado Springs: Waterbrook, 2001), 13.

[5]After I die, I hope I'm made the patron saint of three-day weekends.

[6]Marian Wright Edelmen, *The Measure of Our Success: A Letter to My Children and Yours* (New York: HarperPerennial, 1993), 70.

[7]If this sounds to you like "mindfulness," it is not a coincidence. Try reading Jon Kabat-Zinn's *Full Catastrophe Living: Using the Wisdom of Your Body and Mind to Face Stress, Pain and Illness* (New York: Delacorte Press, 1990).

[8]Richard Rohr, *Everything Belongs: The Gift of Contemplative Prayer* (New York: Crossroad, 2003).

[9]When I hear "spirits," I inevitably think of the three figures that visited Ebenezer Scrooge in *A Christmas Carol* or else what you order at a bar. If you order too many spirits at a bar, you may find yourself visited by three spirits in the middle of the night.

[10]William Ury, *Getting Past No: Negotiating in Difficult Situations* (New York: Bantam, 1993), 39. In context, the author is speaking of unfair debate tactics.

[11]The first time I taught a class in church, as a young seminarian, I taught on the parables. After the second class, which I thought went exceedingly well, an older gentleman came up to the front as everyone left. He had a glint in his eyes, and I readied myself for a compliment, a confirmation of my dazzling spiritual gifts. He smiled, leaned in and said, "You should never put your hands in your pockets when you are teaching." So I knocked his cane out of his hand and ran away. (Not really.)

[12]Deborah Van Deusen Hunsinger, *Pray Without Ceasing: Revitalizing Pastoral Care* (Grand Rapids: Eerdmans, 2006), 86.

[13]Hunsinger, *Pray Without Ceasing*, 95.

[14]I first heard about AHEN when my acquaintance Kara Zimmerman tweeted it. I Googled it, and I can't find anything about it on the Internet, so as far as I know, Kara made it up. Good for you, Kara. It's brilliant.

[15]Richard Foster, *Celebration of Discipline*, 20th Anniversary ed. (San Francisco: HarperSanFrancisco, 1998), 55.

[16]David Benner, "Toxic Spirituality," personal blog, October 20, 2012, www .drdavidgbenner.ca/toxic-spirituality.

[17]Barton, *Invitation to Solitude and Silence*, 60.

[18]Assuming the attraction is consistent with the principles of the Scriptures and the historic confessions of the church.

[19]John Savage, *Listening and Caring Skills in Ministry* (Nashville: Abingdon, 1996), 120.

[20]Rainer Maria Rilke, *Letters to a Young Poet* (Seaside, OR: Merchant Books, 2012), 21.

9: THE SOCIETY OF REVERSE LISTENING

[1]This was at a pub in Irvine, California, in March 2010. I had told Scot I was writing a book about listening, and he said, "That's a really challenging topic to write about. I told my wife you were writing an entire book about listening, and she said 'That sounds really boring.'" It's the encouragement of mentors I have received that has made me who I am today.

[2]This community is called Pomona Hope. See www.pomonahope.org.

[3]Michael Frost, "How to Listen to Your Neighborhood," April 19, 2012, www .vergenetwork.org/2012/04/19/michael-frost-how-to-listen-to-your -neighborhood. He seems to be borrowing from Dr. William Osler, who said, "Listen to your patient, he is telling you the diagnosis."

Also by Adam S. McHugh

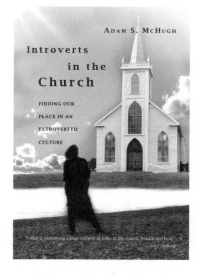

Introverts in the Church
978-0-8308-3702-1